The AI Dilemma:

Exploring the Pros and Cons of Artificial Intelligence

By
Fabio Vescio

Contents

Introduction

Artificial Intelligence (AI) has become one of the most transformative technologies of the modern era. From automating tedious tasks to enhancing medical research, AI is reshaping industries and daily life. However, its rapid advancement also raises ethical, economic, and societal concerns.

This book aims to present a balanced argument, exploring both the advantages and disadvantages of AI.

It aims to provide readers with a comprehensive understanding of AI's dual nature, encouraging informed discussions about its role in our world.

Chapter 1: Understanding AI

Artificial Intelligence (AI) is the simulation of human intelligence in machines that can perform tasks typically requiring human cognition, such as problem-solving, learning, decision-making, language understanding, and perception. AI systems can be designed using rule-based symbolic logic or machine learning models that learn from data. AI is broadly classified into three categories: Narrow AI (Weak AI), which is designed to perform specific tasks, such as virtual assistants like Siri and Alexa; General AI (Strong AI), which is a hypothetical AI with human-like reasoning and problem-solving abilities across multiple domains; and Superintelligent AI, a theoretical concept where AI surpasses human intelligence in all aspects. The history of AI dates back to ancient mythology and early automata, but the foundational theories emerged in the 17th and 18th centuries when philosophers like René Descartes and mathematicians like Gottfried Leibniz proposed theories of mechanical reasoning and symbolic logic. The modern era of AI began in the 1950s when Alan Turing introduced the *Turing Test* as a criterion for determining machine intelligence, and the term "Artificial Intelligence" was coined at the 1956 Dartmouth Conference led by John McCarthy and Marvin Minsky. Early AI programs, such as the Logic Theorist and General Problem Solver, demonstrated AI's potential in problem-solving. However, despite early progress, AI experienced setbacks during the 1970s and 1980s, leading to an "AI Winter" due to funding cuts and limited computing power. During this time, expert systems were developed, mimicking human decision-making in specialized fields, and the LISP programming language became a standard for AI research.

By the 1990s and 2000s, AI research shifted towards data-driven learning with machine learning and neural networks. In 1997, IBM's Deep Blue defeated world chess champion Garry Kasparov, showcasing AI's strategic capabilities. Machine learning models, statistical methods, and early neural networks improved speech recognition and computer vision applications. The explosion of big data and computational advancements in the 2010s led to the rapid rise of deep learning. In 2012, the deep learning revolution took off, powered by neural networks trained on massive datasets, and in 2016, Google's AlphaGo defeated the world's best Go player, demonstrating AI's advanced strategic abilities. AI became widely used in healthcare, finance, self-driving cars, and natural language processing (NLP), with large language models like GPT (Generative Pre-trained Transformer) and BERT transforming AI's role in human communication. Looking ahead, AI research is focused on advancing towards Artificial General Intelligence (AGI), enhancing explainable AI to ensure transparency and ethical considerations, exploring quantum AI and next-generation robotics, and developing AI-human collaboration for safer, more effective integration into society. The future of AI holds limitless potential, promising revolutionary advancements while raising ethical and regulatory questions that must be addressed thoughtfully.

Different Types of AI: Narrow AI vs. General AI

Artificial Intelligence (AI) has transformed various industries and continues to shape the future of technology. There are two primary types of AI: Narrow AI and General AI. Narrow AI, also known as Weak AI, is designed to perform specific tasks efficiently, such as voice recognition, image processing, or recommendation systems. General AI, or Strong AI, represents a more advanced level of artificial intelligence, capable of human-like reasoning and decision-making across a wide range of tasks. While Narrow AI is widely used today in applications like virtual assistants, search engines, and autonomous vehicles, General AI remains a theoretical concept with ongoing research and development efforts aimed at achieving its full potential. Understanding the differences between these two types of AI is essential to grasp the current landscape of AI technology and its future possibilities.

Narrow AI is built to excel at a singular function, and it operates under a pre-defined set of rules and constraints. Examples of Narrow AI include Apple's Siri, Amazon's Alexa, and Google Assistant, which can understand voice commands but do not possess consciousness or independent reasoning. Other instances include image recognition software, spam filters, and self-driving car algorithms that rely on vast amounts of data to function efficiently. Despite their advanced capabilities, these AI systems lack the ability to transfer knowledge from one domain to another, which means they cannot perform tasks outside their designed scope. Narrow AI operates on machine learning algorithms, neural networks, and deep learning techniques that enable pattern recognition and predictive analysis. However, they cannot think, reason, or understand concepts beyond the specific data sets they are trained on. These AI systems are excellent at automation, increasing efficiency, and reducing human effort in repetitive tasks, but they do not exhibit creativity, emotions, or general intelligence.

On the other hand, General AI aims to replicate human cognitive abilities by understanding, learning, and applying knowledge across different domains. Unlike Narrow AI, which is confined to specialized tasks, General AI would possess the ability to reason, plan, solve problems, and adapt to new situations without human intervention. The idea behind General AI is to develop a system that can think like a human, understand abstract concepts, and perform any intellectual task that a human can. This level of AI would require advanced machine learning, cognitive computing, and neural network architectures that mimic the human brain. However, General AI is still in its infancy, with researchers and scientists working on theories and models that could potentially bring it to life. The challenge in achieving General AI lies in developing algorithms that allow machines to exhibit true understanding, consciousness, and self-awareness. While AI researchers have made significant progress in natural language processing, robotics, and machine learning, achieving true General AI remains a distant goal. If realized, General AI could revolutionize industries by performing complex tasks that require creativity, critical thinking, and emotional intelligence, making it a groundbreaking advancement in technology.

In conclusion, the distinction between Narrow AI and General AI highlights the current capabilities and future aspirations of artificial intelligence. Narrow AI is already integrated into various sectors, providing specialized, efficient solutions for specific tasks, while General AI remains a vision that researchers strive to achieve. The development of General AI poses significant technical and ethical challenges, as it would require machines to develop true reasoning, consciousness, and autonomy. Despite the current limitations, ongoing research in AI and machine learning continues to push the boundaries of what is possible, bringing us closer to a future where AI could potentially reach human-like intelligence. As technology advances, understanding the differences between Narrow AI and General AI is crucial for appreciating the impact AI has on society and its potential to transform the world.

Key advancements and current applications

Key advancements in technology and science have significantly shaped modern society, influencing various industries and everyday life. One of the most notable advancements is artificial intelligence (AI), which has transformed multiple sectors, including healthcare, finance, and manufacturing. AI-powered tools, such as machine learning algorithms and natural language processing, have enabled automation, improved decision-making, and enhanced efficiency. In healthcare, AI-driven diagnostic systems assist doctors in detecting diseases like cancer with greater accuracy, while robotic-assisted surgeries have improved precision and patient outcomes. Similarly, in finance, AI is utilized for fraud detection, algorithmic trading, and personalized customer service through chatbots. Moreover, the advent of 5G technology has revolutionized communication by offering faster internet speeds, reduced latency, and enhanced connectivity, supporting innovations like the Internet of Things (IoT) and smart cities. These technological advancements continue to drive progress, creating a more interconnected and efficient world.

In addition to AI and 5G, renewable energy advancements have played a crucial role in addressing climate change and promoting sustainability. Solar and wind energy technologies have seen significant improvements in efficiency and affordability, making them more viable alternatives to fossil fuels. Innovations such as perovskite solar cells and floating wind farms have increased energy production while reducing environmental impact. Furthermore, advancements in battery storage technology, such as solid-state batteries, have improved energy storage capacity, enabling a more stable and reliable renewable energy grid. Electric vehicles (EVs) have also benefited from these advancements, with longer battery life, faster charging times, and increased affordability making them a more practical option for consumers. Governments and private enterprises worldwide are investing heavily in green technologies, aiming to reduce carbon emissions and transition to a more sustainable energy future. The progress in renewable energy not only mitigates environmental concerns but also fosters economic growth through job creation and technological innovation.

The biomedical field has also experienced groundbreaking advancements, particularly in genetic engineering and biotechnology. The development of CRISPR-Cas9 gene-editing technology has revolutionized medicine by allowing scientists to modify genes with unprecedented precision, opening doors for potential cures for genetic disorders, such as sickle cell anemia and cystic fibrosis. Furthermore, advancements in mRNA vaccine technology, as demonstrated by the rapid development of COVID-19 vaccines, have highlighted the potential for combating infectious diseases more effectively. Personalized medicine, powered by genomics and AI, tailors treatments to individual patients based on their genetic makeup, increasing treatment efficacy and minimizing adverse effects. In regenerative medicine, breakthroughs in stem cell research and 3D bioprinting have paved the way for creating lab-grown organs and tissues, offering hope for organ transplant patients. These biomedical innovations continue to push the boundaries of medical science, improving healthcare outcomes and enhancing the quality of life for people worldwide. As research and development efforts continue, the potential applications of these advancements will expand, shaping the future of medicine and beyond.

Chapter 2: The Benefits of AI

Increased Efficiency and Automation:

AI reduces human workload by performing repetitive tasks faster and more accurately.

Increased Efficiency and Automation: AI reduces human workload by performing repetitive tasks faster and more accurately.

Artificial intelligence (AI) has revolutionized efficiency and automation across various industries, significantly reducing human workload while enhancing productivity. AI-powered systems excel at handling repetitive and mundane tasks with greater speed and precision, allowing employees to focus on more complex and strategic activities. In manufacturing, AI-driven robotic process automation (RPA) streamlines assembly lines by performing tasks such as quality control, packaging, and material handling with minimal human intervention. This leads to increased production rates, reduced errors, and lower operational costs. Similarly, in business operations, AI automates data entry, document processing, and customer service through chatbots, significantly improving efficiency and reducing the need for manual labour. These advancements have transformed workflows, optimizing resource utilization and enabling organizations to achieve higher output with less effort.

The impact of AI-driven automation extends beyond manufacturing and business processes to sectors such as healthcare, logistics, and finance. In healthcare, AI-powered diagnostic tools analyse medical images, detect diseases, and generate reports with remarkable accuracy, assisting doctors in making informed decisions and reducing diagnostic errors. Robotic surgical systems perform delicate procedures with unparalleled precision, minimizing recovery time for patients. In logistics, AI optimizes supply chain management by predicting demand, automating warehouse operations, and improving route planning, leading to faster deliveries and cost savings.

Financial institutions leverage AI for fraud detection, risk assessment, and algorithmic trading, ensuring enhanced security and efficiency in transactions. These applications demonstrate how AI-driven automation enhances accuracy, speed, and scalability across diverse industries.

As AI continues to evolve, the potential for increased efficiency and automation will only expand, driving further innovations and reshaping the future of work. With advancements in machine learning and natural language processing, AI systems are becoming more intelligent, capable of handling complex decision-making processes and adapting to new challenges. While automation may replace some traditional jobs, it also creates opportunities for new roles that require human creativity, problem-solving, and oversight of AI systems. Organizations must balance automation with workforce development, ensuring employees are equipped with the necessary skills to work alongside AI. Ethical considerations, such as data privacy, bias in AI algorithms, and job displacement, must also be addressed to ensure responsible AI deployment. As industries continue to integrate AI-driven automation, the focus should remain on harnessing its potential to improve productivity while maintaining a human-centric approach to innovation and progress.

Medical Breakthroughs:

AI assists in diagnosing diseases, drug discovery, and personalized treatments.

Artificial intelligence (AI) is revolutionizing the medical field by significantly improving the accuracy and speed of diagnosing diseases, accelerating drug discovery, and enabling personalized treatments. With the integration of machine learning algorithms, neural networks, and big data analytics, AI is reshaping the way healthcare professionals detect, analyse, and treat a variety of medical conditions. One of the most prominent applications of AI in healthcare is disease diagnosis. Traditional diagnostic methods often rely on time-consuming tests and human interpretation, which can lead to delays or errors. AI-powered systems, however, can analyse vast amounts of medical data, including imaging scans, lab results, and genetic information, to detect diseases with remarkable precision. For instance, AI algorithms have been shown to outperform radiologists in detecting cancers such as breast and lung cancer by analysing medical images for early signs of malignancy. Additionally, AI models are being developed to predict the onset of diseases such as Alzheimer's and Parkinson's by identifying patterns in patient data long before symptoms appear. This early detection enables timely intervention and improves patient outcomes.

Another groundbreaking area where AI is making a significant impact is drug discovery. The traditional process of developing new medications is notoriously lengthy, costly, and complex, often taking over a decade and billions of dollars to bring a single drug to market. AI-driven drug discovery aims to streamline this process by utilizing advanced algorithms to analyse vast datasets of chemical compounds, biological interactions, and genetic information. AI can identify potential drug candidates, predict their efficacy, and optimize molecular structures for better therapeutic outcomes. For example, AI has been instrumental in the rapid development of COVID-19 treatments and vaccines by analysing viral structures and identifying promising drug targets at an unprecedented speed. Additionally, pharmaceutical companies are leveraging AI to repurpose existing drugs for new therapeutic applications, thereby reducing costs and accelerating treatment availability. By automating many aspects of drug discovery, AI not only enhances efficiency but also opens doors to innovative treatments for rare and complex diseases that have long been challenging to address through traditional research methods.

Personalized medicine is another transformative area where AI is making a profound difference. Traditional treatment approaches often follow a one-size-fits-all model, which may not always be effective for every patient due to genetic and lifestyle variations. AI enables precision medicine by analysing individual patient data, including genetic profiles, medical histories, and lifestyle factors, to tailor treatments specifically to each person's unique needs. Machine learning models can predict how a patient will respond to a particular drug or therapy, allowing doctors to select the most effective treatment with minimal side effects. In oncology, for example, AI-driven genomic analysis helps identify genetic mutations driving cancer growth and recommends targeted therapies that are most likely to succeed. Furthermore, wearable AI-powered devices continuously monitor patients' vital signs and health metrics, alerting healthcare providers to potential complications before they become critical. This real-time data analysis empowers both patients and doctors to make informed decisions about treatment adjustments, leading to improved health outcomes and reduced hospitalizations. As AI continues to evolve, its potential to revolutionize medical breakthroughs is limitless, offering hope for more accurate diagnoses, faster drug development, and truly personalized healthcare solutions.

Enhanced Decision-Making: AI Analyses Large Datasets to Help Businesses and Governments Make Informed Decisions

Artificial Intelligence (AI) has revolutionized decision-making processes across industries by analysing vast amounts of data to provide valuable insights. Businesses and governments increasingly rely on AI to enhance efficiency, accuracy, and strategic planning. The ability of AI to process large datasets at unprecedented speeds enables organizations to make data-driven decisions that improve productivity, reduce costs, and mitigate risks. By leveraging AI-driven analytics, decision-makers can optimize resource allocation, enhance customer experiences, and address complex challenges in real-time. The integration of AI into decision-making frameworks ensures that data is utilized effectively, allowing organizations to remain competitive and adaptable in an ever-changing global landscape.

In the business world, AI-powered decision-making offers significant advantages, particularly in areas such as financial forecasting, marketing, and operations management. Companies utilize AI algorithms to analyse consumer behaviour, market trends, and economic indicators, enabling them to develop targeted strategies that drive growth. For instance, AI-driven predictive analytics help businesses forecast demand, optimize supply chains, and enhance inventory management, reducing waste and improving efficiency. Additionally, AI assists in risk management by identifying fraudulent activities, monitoring cybersecurity threats, and detecting anomalies in financial transactions. Businesses also employ AI-driven chatbots and virtual assistants to enhance customer service by providing personalized recommendations and support. By leveraging AI's data processing capabilities, organizations can make informed decisions that lead to increased profitability, customer satisfaction, and operational excellence.

Governments also benefit from AI-driven decision-making in areas such as public policy, healthcare, and infrastructure development. AI enables policymakers to analyse demographic data, economic trends, and social behaviours, allowing them to formulate effective policies that address societal needs. For example, AI-powered systems assist in predicting and managing public health crises by analysing epidemiological data and identifying patterns of disease outbreaks. This capability was particularly evident during the COVID-19 pandemic when AI models helped governments track virus transmission, allocate medical resources, and develop containment strategies. Furthermore, AI aids in urban planning by optimizing traffic management, improving energy efficiency, and enhancing public transportation systems. Law enforcement agencies use AI to analyse crime patterns, predict potential threats, and deploy resources more effectively. By utilizing AI for evidence-based policymaking, governments can enhance public services, improve governance, and ensure the well-being of citizens.

One of the most transformative applications of AI in decision-making is in the field of big data analytics. AI-powered systems can process massive amounts of structured and unstructured data, identifying patterns and correlations that human analysts might overlook. Machine learning algorithms continuously refine their predictions by learning from new data, improving accuracy over time. AI-driven analytics enable organizations to perform scenario analysis, simulate outcomes, and assess potential risks before making crucial decisions. In finance, for instance, AI-powered investment models analyse market data, investor sentiment, and macroeconomic indicators to optimize portfolio management and minimize financial risks. Similarly, AI assists healthcare professionals by analysing patient data, predicting disease progression, and recommending personalized treatment plans. By harnessing the power of AI in big data analytics, organizations can make proactive and informed decisions that lead to better outcomes.

Despite its numerous advantages, AI-driven decision-making also presents challenges that need to be addressed. One of the primary concerns is data bias, where AI algorithms may produce biased outcomes if the training data is not representative of diverse populations. This issue can lead to unfair treatment and unintended consequences, particularly in sectors such as hiring, lending, and law enforcement. Ensuring transparency and fairness in AI models requires rigorous testing, diverse datasets, and ongoing monitoring to mitigate biases. Another challenge is data privacy and security, as AI relies on vast amounts of sensitive information to generate insights. Organizations must implement robust cybersecurity measures to protect data from breaches and unauthorized access. Additionally, ethical considerations surrounding AI decision-making, such as accountability and explainability, need to be addressed to build trust among stakeholders. By developing ethical AI frameworks and regulatory guidelines, businesses and governments can ensure responsible AI deployment in decision-making processes.

The future of AI-driven decision-making holds immense potential as advancements in AI technologies continue to evolve. Emerging trends such as explainable AI (XAI), quantum computing, and edge AI are expected to further enhance decision-making capabilities. Explainable AI aims to make AI models more interpretable, allowing decision-makers to understand the reasoning behind AI-generated insights. This transparency is crucial for regulatory compliance and ethical considerations. Quantum computing, with its ability to process complex computations at unprecedented speeds, is poised to revolutionize AI-driven analytics, enabling organizations to solve complex problems more efficiently. Edge AI, which processes data closer to the source rather than relying on centralized cloud computing, enhances real-time decision-making in critical applications such as autonomous vehicles and industrial automation. As these technologies advance, AI-driven decision-making will become more sophisticated, empowering organizations to navigate challenges and seize opportunities in an increasingly data-driven world.

In conclusion, AI's ability to analyse large datasets has transformed decision-making for businesses and governments, enabling them to make informed, data-driven choices. From optimizing business operations and enhancing customer experiences to improving public policy and urban planning, AI-driven analytics play a crucial role in shaping the future of industries and societies. However, challenges such as data bias, privacy concerns, and ethical considerations must be addressed to ensure responsible AI deployment. As AI technologies continue to evolve, organizations that embrace AI-driven decision-making will gain a competitive edge, improve efficiency, and drive innovation in a rapidly changing global landscape.

Economic Growth: AI-Driven Automation Leads to Cost Savings and Productivity Boosts

Artificial intelligence (AI) and automation are revolutionizing industries worldwide, driving significant economic growth by enhancing productivity and reducing operational costs. The adoption of AI-driven automation streamlines processes, reduces human error, and increases efficiency across various sectors. Companies that integrate AI into their operations benefit from increased output, lower production costs, and enhanced innovation. By automating repetitive and time-consuming tasks, businesses can allocate resources more effectively, fostering economic expansion and improving competitiveness in global markets.

One of the primary ways AI-driven automation contributes to economic growth is through substantial cost savings. Businesses leveraging AI technologies can optimize workflows and minimize labour costs by automating routine tasks. For instance, in manufacturing, robotic process automation (RPA) enables companies to reduce the need for manual labour while maintaining high levels of precision and speed. Similarly, AI-driven chatbots and virtual assistants in customer service industries significantly lower operational expenses by handling inquiries without human intervention. Additionally, AI-powered predictive maintenance in industries such as aviation, logistics, and energy prevent costly equipment failures, thereby reducing downtime and maintenance expenses. These cost-saving measures translate into higher profitability for businesses and contribute to overall economic expansion.

Beyond cost savings, AI-driven automation enhances productivity by allowing organizations to accomplish more with fewer resources. AI algorithms process vast amounts of data rapidly, providing businesses with valuable insights for decision-making. For example, in finance, AI-driven analytics help detect fraudulent transactions and streamline investment strategies, leading to improved financial performance. In healthcare, AI-powered diagnostic tools enable faster and more accurate disease detection, reducing the burden on medical professionals and improving patient outcomes. Similarly, AI-based supply chain management solutions optimize inventory levels, reduce waste, and ensure timely deliveries, enhancing overall operational efficiency. As industries continue to embrace AI automation, productivity gains translate into increased economic output, fuelling sustained growth and development.

Moreover, AI-driven automation fosters innovation, creating new business opportunities and driving economic transformation. Companies investing in AI research and development (R&D) gain a competitive advantage by pioneering new products, services, and business models. Startups leveraging AI technologies disrupt traditional industries, generating employment opportunities and stimulating economic activity. For instance, autonomous vehicles and smart logistics solutions are reshaping the transportation industry, reducing costs, and improving efficiency. AI-powered software development tools accelerate coding processes, enabling companies to bring innovative applications to market faster. Additionally, AI-driven personalized marketing strategies enhance customer engagement and boost sales, contributing to overall economic prosperity. As AI continues to evolve, its role in fostering innovation will be a key driver of economic growth in the digital era.

Despite its numerous benefits, AI-driven automation also raises concerns regarding job displacement and workforce adaptation. While automation reduces the demand for certain manual and repetitive tasks, it simultaneously creates demand for new skill sets. To mitigate the risks of job displacement, businesses and governments must invest in reskilling and upskilling programs. Educational institutions must adapt curricula to equip students with AI-related competencies, preparing them for the evolving job market. Additionally, policymakers should implement strategies to support workers transitioning into AI-driven industries, ensuring inclusive economic growth. By addressing these challenges, societies can maximize the benefits of AI automation while minimizing potential disruptions to the labour market.

In conclusion, AI-driven automation plays a pivotal role in driving economic growth by reducing costs, enhancing productivity, and fostering innovation. Businesses that embrace AI technologies gain a competitive edge, optimize operations, and create new economic opportunities. While the transition to an AI-powered economy presents challenges, proactive measures in education and workforce development can ensure sustainable growth. As AI continues to evolve, its impact on economic expansion will be profound, shaping the future of industries and global markets.

Improved Safety and Security: AI-powered Surveillance, Cybersecurity, and Predictive Analytics Enhance Safety

The intersection of artificial intelligence (AI) and safety has revolutionized how we protect individuals, organizations, and nations. With the increasing complexity of threats and the rapid pace of technological evolution, AI-powered solutions have become critical in enhancing safety and security across various sectors. AI is now integrated into surveillance systems, cybersecurity measures, and predictive analytics, each of which plays a pivotal role in safeguarding lives, assets, and information. The following discussion explores how AI improves safety and security, offering a deeper look into AI-powered surveillance, cybersecurity, and predictive analytics, all of which work synergistically to create a safer environment for society at large.

AI-Powered Surveillance

One of the most prominent applications of AI in safety is its role in surveillance systems. Traditional surveillance methods, including the use of CCTV cameras, have long been crucial in monitoring public and private spaces. However, AI has transformed these systems by adding capabilities that allow for real-time analysis, greater accuracy, and proactive responses to potential security threats. Through computer vision and machine learning algorithms, AI can automatically analyse video footage, identify suspicious behaviour, detect anomalies, and even recognize faces or objects. This is a significant improvement over manual surveillance, where human operators must sift through hours of footage, often missing critical events or failing to respond promptly.

AI-powered surveillance systems can track individuals or vehicles across different camera feeds, creating a comprehensive overview of movements within an area. This allows law enforcement agencies, security personnel, and organizations to respond to incidents in real-time, improving the speed and effectiveness of interventions. Moreover, these systems can alert authorities to suspicious activities, such as unauthorized access to restricted areas or unusual patterns of behaviour, prompting immediate investigation. Additionally, AI surveillance systems are also capable of operating in low-light or challenging environments, providing enhanced coverage and reliability that traditional methods often cannot match.

Facial recognition is another powerful application of AI in surveillance, helping law enforcement and security teams identify individuals in crowded spaces or restricted areas. While there are ethical concerns surrounding privacy and potential misuse of facial recognition, its potential to improve public safety is undeniable. AI can cross-reference individuals with databases of known criminals, missing persons, or persons of interest, enabling rapid identification and reducing the risk of security breaches.

Cybersecurity: Protecting Digital Assets

As the world becomes increasingly digital, cybersecurity has become an essential aspect of safety and security. AI plays a transformative role in fortifying cybersecurity systems by enabling faster threat detection, more accurate predictions of potential breaches, and automated responses to cyberattacks. The constant evolution of cyber threats, from phishing attacks to advanced persistent threats (APTs), has created a critical need for AI-driven security tools capable of adapting to these ever-changing risks.

AI's ability to analyse vast amounts of data in real-time allows it to detect potential cyber threats much faster than human analysts. Traditional cybersecurity methods often rely on signature-based detection, which involves searching for known patterns of malicious activity. However, this approach has limitations as cybercriminals continuously adapt their tactics to evade detection. AI-powered systems, on the other hand, can learn from vast datasets, identify patterns, and detect anomalies that might indicate a breach. For example, machine learning algorithms can identify abnormal user behaviours, such as unauthorized access to sensitive files or unusual login times, which could signify a potential attack.

Furthermore, AI can be employed in threat prediction, where predictive analytics models assess the likelihood of future cyberattacks based on current and past data. This enables organizations to take proactive measures, such as strengthening vulnerable systems, improving firewalls, or educating employees about emerging phishing scams. By predicting and mitigating threats before they occur, AI is fundamentally changing how organizations approach cybersecurity, shifting from a reactive to a proactive stance.

One of the most innovative AI applications in cybersecurity is automated response. In the event of a detected threat, AI systems can autonomously take actions such as isolating compromised devices, blocking malicious IP addresses, or alerting human administrators for further intervention. This speed is critical in preventing the spread of cyberattacks and minimizing damage. AI can also adapt to new threats over time, learning from past incidents and continuously improving its responses. This adaptive capability makes AI an invaluable tool for organizations facing increasingly sophisticated and diverse cyber threats.

Predictive Analytics: Foreseeing and Preventing Potential Threats

In addition to AI's role in surveillance and cybersecurity, predictive analytics represents another significant area where AI enhances safety and security. Predictive analytics uses AI algorithms and historical data to forecast potential risks, enabling organizations to take pre-emptive action and avoid adverse outcomes. In the realm of safety, this technology has been particularly transformative in fields such as disaster management, public health, and criminal justice.

38

For example, AI-powered predictive analytics can be applied to disaster management by analysing historical weather patterns, seismic data, and other environmental factors to predict natural disasters such as hurricanes, floods, or earthquakes. By accurately forecasting these events, AI systems enable authorities to issue timely warnings, evacuate vulnerable areas, and allocate resources where they are most needed, ultimately saving lives and reducing property damage. Similarly, predictive analytics can be used to optimize the deployment of emergency services, ensuring a swift and coordinated response to incidents.

In public health, AI-driven predictive models can help anticipate disease outbreaks or epidemics, enabling governments and healthcare organizations to take preventive measures before a full-blown crisis occurs. For example, AI can analyse patterns in healthcare data, such as the spread of infectious diseases or the emergence of new pathogens, to predict where and when outbreaks are most likely to occur. By leveraging this information, public health authorities can mobilize resources, implement containment strategies, and issue advisories to protect public health.

Predictive analytics is also a powerful tool in crime prevention. By analysing crime data, AI algorithms can identify trends and patterns in criminal behaviour, helping law enforcement agencies predict where and when crimes are most likely to occur. This information allows for the strategic placement of officers, improving response times and preventing criminal activity before it happens. Additionally, predictive analytics can be used to assess the risk of reoffending in individuals involved in the criminal justice system, enabling more targeted interventions and reducing the likelihood of recidivism.

Conclusion

In conclusion, AI-powered surveillance, cybersecurity, and predictive analytics are transforming the landscape of safety and security in profound ways. The integration of AI into surveillance systems enhances the ability to detect and respond to potential threats in real-time, offering unprecedented levels of monitoring and protection. In cybersecurity, AI plays a critical role in defending digital assets against increasingly sophisticated attacks by enabling rapid threat detection, prediction, and automated response. Finally, predictive analytics allows for the anticipation of potential risks, giving organizations the foresight to act proactively in preventing disasters, health crises, or criminal activities. Together, these AI-driven technologies are not only improving the safety and security of individuals and organizations but also reshaping the future of how we protect ourselves and our communities in an increasingly interconnected world. As AI continues to evolve, its role in ensuring safety and security will only expand, offering new opportunities for prevention, intervention, and the creation of safer environments for all.

Chapter 3: The Drawbacks of AI

Job Displacement and Economic Inequality: Automation threatens jobs, especially in manufacturing and service sectors.

Job displacement and economic inequality have been significant issues in the context of technological advancements, particularly the rise of automation. Automation refers to the use of machinery, robotics, artificial intelligence (AI), and other technology to perform tasks that were traditionally carried out by human workers. Over the past few decades, the rapid pace of innovation has introduced automation in industries ranging from manufacturing to service sectors. While automation has undoubtedly improved productivity, efficiency, and reduced costs for businesses, it has also led to widespread job displacement, particularly among low-skilled and middle-skilled workers. As machines and algorithms take over repetitive or dangerous tasks, human workers are increasingly being pushed out of traditional employment roles, resulting in major socioeconomic implications.

Manufacturing has been one of the most affected sectors by automation. Historically, manufacturing jobs provided stable employment opportunities for millions of workers in countries like the United States, Germany, and China. These jobs often required some skill but were accessible to individuals with limited education or training. However, the introduction of robots, automated production lines, and AI-driven processes has revolutionized this sector, reducing the need for human labour. Machines can now perform tasks such as assembly, inspection, and packaging more efficiently and accurately than humans. This shift has led to significant job losses, particularly in regions that were once dependent on manufacturing industries. For instance, areas in the Rust Belt in the United States, where large factories once employed thousands, have seen severe declines in employment due to automation.

In addition to the displacement of workers, automation in manufacturing also contributes to growing economic inequality. Many of the jobs that automation eliminates are low-wage, manual labour positions, while the new opportunities that emerge tend to be in high-tech fields that require specialized skills. This shift exacerbates the wage gap between skilled and unskilled workers. Those with advanced education or expertise in fields like robotics, AI, or data science are able to command high salaries, while those displaced by automation may struggle to find new work that offers comparable pay. Consequently, automation has widened the economic divide between workers in different skill categories. Workers without the necessary training or education to transition to high-tech jobs are often left behind, further entrenching inequality in society.

The service sector has also experienced significant disruptions due to automation. The advent of self-checkout machines, AI-driven customer service representatives, and delivery robots has replaced many traditional roles in retail, food services, and customer support. Jobs that once required human interaction, such as cashiers, clerks, or telemarketers, are increasingly being automated, leading to job displacement for millions of workers. Furthermore, the rise of gig economy platforms, such as Uber, Lyft, and food delivery services, has created a labour market where workers are often employed on a temporary or part-time basis with limited benefits. Automation in this context tends to replace full-time positions with part-time or freelance work, further destabilizing income security for many workers.

This shift in the workforce is not without its social consequences. In regions heavily reliant on low-wage, service sector jobs, such as fast food restaurants and retail outlets, large-scale automation may lead to significant unemployment or underemployment. This has implications not only for individual workers but also for the broader economy. Displaced workers may face difficulty in finding new employment, particularly in areas where access to training and education opportunities is limited. As a result, many people who lose their jobs due to automation may face long-term unemployment, which can lead to increased poverty and social unrest. Those left behind in an increasingly automated economy are often forced to rely on government assistance or other social safety nets, placing a strain on public resources.

The shift towards automation and the displacement of workers also contribute to a broader cultural and political divide. The erosion of traditional manufacturing and service sector jobs has fuelled discontent and a sense of alienation among those who feel left behind by globalization and technological change. This sense of disenfranchisement has played a role in political movements and populist rhetoric that promises to restore lost jobs and protect workers from the negative effects of automation. The rise of such movements underscores the social tensions that arise when large portions of the workforce face job insecurity and economic instability. Automation, while driving innovation and economic growth in certain sectors, has raised fundamental questions about the future of work and the role of government in ensuring that technological progress benefits everyone, not just a select few.

There is also a growing debate about how to address the challenges posed by automation in terms of both job displacement and economic inequality. Some advocates argue that the key to mitigating the negative effects of automation is through education and retraining programs. These initiatives would help displaced workers acquire new skills and transition into sectors less vulnerable to automation, such as healthcare, renewable energy, or advanced technology fields. Governments, businesses, and educational institutions have a critical role to play in facilitating this transition. For example, community colleges, vocational schools, and online learning platforms can offer affordable retraining programs that equip workers with the skills needed in an automated economy.

However, others argue that more radical solutions are necessary to address the deepening economic inequality caused by automation. One such solution is the implementation of a Universal Basic Income (UBI), a policy that provides all citizens with a guaranteed income regardless of employment status. UBI advocates argue that in a world where automation is increasingly displacing workers, providing a basic income could help cushion the impact of job loss and reduce poverty. By ensuring a stable source of income for everyone, UBI could help reduce the financial strain on workers displaced by automation and allow them to focus on retraining or pursuing other opportunities. However, the feasibility of UBI remains a contentious issue, with concerns about its cost and potential effects on labour markets.

In conclusion, automation is reshaping the job market in profound ways, with manufacturing and service sectors being particularly vulnerable to job displacement. While automation offers significant benefits in terms of efficiency and productivity, it also exacerbates economic inequality by eliminating low-wage jobs and creating a divide between skilled and unskilled workers. The displacement of workers by machines has social and political consequences, fuelling discontent and highlighting the need for thoughtful policies to address the challenges posed by automation. Whether through education and retraining programs or more radical approaches such as Universal Basic Income, finding ways to mitigate the negative effects of automation will be crucial in ensuring that the benefits of technological advancement are shared more equitably across society.

Ethical Concerns: Issues related to bias, surveillance, and misuse of AI.

Artificial Intelligence (AI) has seen exponential growth in recent years, advancing in fields ranging from healthcare to autonomous vehicles. While AI has the potential to revolutionize industries and improve lives, its rapid development raises several ethical concerns, particularly regarding issues of bias, surveillance, and misuse. As AI systems are increasingly integrated into everyday life, it is crucial to critically examine how these technologies are being developed, deployed, and governed, as well as the potential harms they may cause to individuals, communities, and societies at large.

Bias in AI Systems

One of the most pressing ethical concerns with AI is the issue of bias. AI systems learn patterns from the data they are trained on, and if that data is biased, the resulting AI models can perpetuate and even amplify these biases. This problem is particularly significant in areas such as hiring, law enforcement, healthcare, and lending. For instance, facial recognition technologies have been shown to have higher error rates for people of colour and women, leading to potential misidentifications and unfair treatment. In the context of hiring algorithms, AI may Favor candidates from specific demographic groups, reinforcing gender, racial, or socioeconomic disparities.

Bias in AI systems is often a reflection of historical inequalities embedded in the data used to train them. For example, if an AI system is trained on a dataset of job applicants that disproportionately includes male candidates, the system may unconsciously learn to Favor male applicants over female ones, even if this is not explicitly intended by the designers. Similarly, AI systems trained on historical crime data may perpetuate discriminatory policing practices, disproportionately targeting marginalized communities. This highlights the need for more diverse, representative, and unbiased datasets, as well as transparency in AI development processes to ensure that algorithms are fair and do not reproduce harmful stereotypes or systemic inequalities.

To mitigate bias, there have been calls for AI researchers and developers to implement fairness audits and ethical review processes in the design and deployment of AI systems. This includes ensuring that data used in training models is diverse, representative, and free from bias, as well as developing algorithms that are explicitly designed to detect and correct for bias. In addition, there is growing interest in explainable AI (XAI), which aims to make AI models more transparent and interpretable, allowing stakeholders to understand how decisions are made and identify potential biases.

Surveillance and Privacy Concerns

Another major ethical concern surrounding AI is its potential to infringe on privacy through surveillance. With the growing integration of AI into surveillance technologies, such as facial recognition systems, smart cameras, and data analytics, there is an increasing risk of widespread surveillance, both by governments and private entities. While these technologies can provide benefits, such as enhanced security or crime prevention, they also pose significant risks to personal privacy and civil liberties.

One of the most concerning aspects of AI-enabled surveillance is the ability to track individuals' movements, behaviours, and activities on a massive scale. For example, facial recognition systems are being used by governments and corporations to monitor public spaces, identify individuals in crowds, and even track people's activities across various locations. This has raised concerns about the erosion of privacy, the chilling effect on free speech and assembly, and the potential for abuse by authoritarian regimes. In some countries, AI-driven surveillance has been used to target political dissidents, activists, and minority groups, raising fears of government overreach and the suppression of dissent.

The use of AI in surveillance also raises questions about the extent to which individuals' personal data is being collected, stored, and shared. Many AI s intended consequences.

Moreover, AI technologies can be used for malicious purposes in other areas, such as cyberattacks, disinformation campaigns, and fraud. For instance, AI-generated deepfakes—hyper-realistic videos or audio recordings that manipulate reality—have been used to spread false information, manipulate public opinion, and damage reputations. In the political sphere, AI-powered bots and algorithms are increasingly used to sway elections and influence political discourse by amplifying certain voices or spreading propaganda. The ability to manipulate information on such a large scale undermines trust in democratic institutions and jeopardizes the integrity of the public discourse.

AI is also vulnerable to exploitation in the realm of data privacy and security. Hackers and malicious actors can exploit AI systems to conduct large-scale data breaches, steal sensitive information, or bypass security measures. AI can be used to identify vulnerabilities in networks, create personalized phishing attacks, or develop advanced malware that evades traditional security defences. This not only jeopardizes the security of individuals' personal data but also threatens national security and the stability of critical infrastructure.

To address the potential for AI misuse, there is a growing demand for international cooperation and regulation. Many experts advocate for the development of global agreements and frameworks to govern the use of AI in military, political, and security contexts. Additionally, there is an emphasis on ensuring that AI systems are designed with safeguards that prevent misuse and that they can be audited and held accountable in cases of unethical or malicious use. Ethical AI development must prioritize safety, transparency, and accountability to ensure that these powerful technologies are used responsibly and for the benefit of society.

Conclusion

As AI continues to evolve and become more integrated into society, it is essential to address the ethical concerns surrounding bias, surveillance, and misuse. The potential risks posed by AI—such as perpetuating discrimination, infringing on privacy, and enabling malicious uses—demand careful consideration and thoughtful regulation. Developing fair, transparent, and accountable AI systems requires collaboration among governments, industry leaders, and the public to ensure that AI is used in ways that promote equity, justice, and human dignity. By confronting these ethical challenges head-on, society can harness the benefits of AI while minimizing its potential harms.

surveillance systems rely on large databases of personal information, which can be vulnerable to breaches, misuse, or exploitation. For instance, data harvested by facial recognition systems could be sold to third-party companies for marketing purposes or used by law enforcement to monitor individuals without their knowledge or consent. This creates a dangerous precedent for the normalization of surveillance and the potential for mass surveillance to become an everyday part of life, without adequate safeguards or public oversight.

To address these concerns, advocates for privacy rights have called for stronger regulations around the use of AI in surveillance, including stricter data protection laws and limitations on the deployment of AI surveillance technologies. There is also a growing movement to ban or restrict the use of facial recognition systems in public spaces, as well as to ensure that individuals have more control over their personal data and the ways it is collected and used. Privacy-conscious AI development is essential to strike a balance between the benefits of AI and the protection of individual rights.

Misuse of AI

The potential for the misuse of AI is another critical ethical issue that cannot be overlooked. While AI can be a powerful tool for positive change, it can also be weaponized or manipulated for malicious purposes. One of the most alarming examples of AI misuse is the development of autonomous weapons, also known as "killer robots." These AI-powered machines could be used in military conflicts to identify and engage targets without human intervention. The prospect of machines making life-or-death decisions raises profound ethical questions about accountability, responsibility, and the potential use for war.

Dependence on AI: Overreliance on AI could weaken human skills and judgment.

In the 21st century, artificial intelligence (AI) has emerged as one of the most transformative technologies in human history. From self-driving cars to sophisticated algorithms that drive business decisions, AI is becoming an integral part of everyday life. Its rapid advancements promise significant improvements in efficiency, convenience, and productivity. However, the growing reliance on AI also raises crucial concerns, particularly about its potential to weaken human skills and judgment. The overuse of AI systems could lead to a gradual erosion of essential human abilities that are necessary for decision-making, critical thinking, creativity, and problem-solving. While AI excels in tasks that require pattern recognition, data analysis, and automation, it is not equipped to replicate the complexities of human experience, emotion, and intuition. The more we delegate responsibilities to AI, the more we risk losing the essential cognitive and social abilities that make us human.

One of the most immediate and noticeable effects of overreliance on AI is the gradual decline of critical thinking and decision-making skills. For example, AI-powered systems are increasingly being used in sectors such as healthcare, finance, and law to provide recommendations or make decisions based on vast datasets. While these systems can often outperform human experts in terms of processing speed and accuracy, they lack the nuanced understanding that human judgment brings to the table. In healthcare, for instance, an AI system might suggest the most statistically probable diagnosis based on medical data, but it cannot consider the broader context of a patient's unique circumstances, such as their psychological well-being, family history, or personal values. When human professionals begin to overly depend on AI's recommendations without critically evaluating them, they may lose the ability to make informed, empathetic, and context-aware decisions. In other words, AI may make decisions that are technically sound but lack the human touch that is essential in many professions. This kind of dependence ultimately dulls the skillset of the individuals who use AI, as they become accustomed to deferring to machines rather than relying on their own experience, intuition, and expertise.

The erosion of human skills due to AI overreliance also extends to problem-solving and creativity. While AI systems are incredibly proficient at solving specific problems, they are typically designed to work within predefined parameters and rules. They can analyse vast amounts of data and offer solutions based on patterns they detect, but they lack the ability to think outside the box, innovate, or adapt to unstructured situations. Human problem-solving often involves not only logical reasoning but also the ability to incorporate intuition, imagination, and abstract thinking. Creativity, which is one of humanity's greatest strengths, thrives on ambiguity and the willingness to challenge assumptions and explore new possibilities. However, when individuals over-rely on AI to solve complex problems or generate ideas, they risk stifling their creative thinking and becoming passive consumers of AI-driven solutions rather than active creators and innovators. Over time, this could lead to a generation of individuals who are less capable of original thought and innovation, further eroding the human ability to think critically and creatively.

Furthermore, the overuse of AI in decision-making processes has the potential to erode individual autonomy and judgment. As AI systems become increasingly integrated into daily life, many people may begin to trust these systems more than their own judgment. For example, in areas such as driving, navigation, or even personal finance, individuals may rely on AI-driven recommendations without considering the potential consequences or alternatives. The convenience of AI can be so alluring that it becomes tempting to delegate more and more decisions to machines, even in areas where human experience and intuition are crucial. Over time, this shift in decision-making power could lead to a diminishing sense of personal agency and independence. People might begin to feel less confident in their own abilities to make choices or solve problems without consulting an AI. As a result, they may become overly dependent on technology, undermining their sense of self-reliance and critical thinking skills.

Another major concern is that overreliance on AI could lead to a loss of essential social and emotional skills. In many domains, AI is being designed to replicate or assist with human interactions, such as customer service chatbots, virtual assistants, and even AI therapists. While these technologies can provide convenience and efficiency, they lack the emotional intelligence and empathy that are inherent in human interactions. The use of AI in place of human connection could lead to a decline in face-to-face communication and interpersonal skills. People might become accustomed to interacting with machines rather than with other humans, leading to feelings of isolation and emotional detachment. For instance, AI-driven virtual assistants may answer questions or complete tasks, but they cannot offer the emotional support or understanding that a human would in times of crisis. Over time, this could lead to individuals becoming more disconnected from others, weakening their social bonds and reducing their ability to empathize with others' experiences.

Moreover, the overreliance on AI could exacerbate issues related to privacy and security. As AI systems become increasingly embedded in everyday life, they have access to vast amounts of personal data, such as health records, financial transactions, and even private communications. The more individuals rely on AI to manage their lives, the more data they generate and share with these systems. This dependence raises significant concerns about data security, privacy breaches, and the potential for AI systems to be manipulated or hacked. In a world where AI is trusted to make critical decisions, the consequences of a security failure or system malfunction could be devastating. For example, an AI-driven algorithm responsible for managing financial investments could malfunction, leading to significant financial loss for individuals who rely on it without understanding the underlying processes. Furthermore, as AI systems become more autonomous, individuals may feel less inclined to question the decisions they make or understand how their personal data is being used. This passive trust in AI systems could lead to a loss of awareness about how technology is shaping their lives, making them more vulnerable to exploitation.

In conclusion, while AI has the potential to revolutionize industries, improve efficiency, and solve complex problems, its growing presence also poses significant risks to human skills and judgment. Overreliance on AI can lead to the erosion of critical thinking, creativity, social skills, and personal autonomy. As AI continues to evolve, it is essential for individuals to strike a balance between utilizing its capabilities and maintaining the skills that define human intelligence. To avoid becoming overly dependent on AI, people must remain conscious of the limitations of technology and ensure that it serves as a tool to augment human abilities rather than replace them. By fostering an awareness of these risks, we can work toward a future where AI enhances, rather than diminishes, our unique human capabilities.

Privacy Risks: AI-powered data collection raises concerns about user privacy and consent.

In the digital age, artificial intelligence (AI) has revolutionized how data is collected, processed, and utilized. AI-powered systems have the capability to gather and analyse vast amounts of personal information from various sources, such as social media, browsing history, transaction records, and even physical interactions. While AI promises significant benefits in terms of efficiency, personalized services, and automation, its ability to collect data at such an unprecedented scale has raised serious concerns about user privacy and consent. As AI technologies become more integrated into everyday life, understanding the privacy risks associated with these technologies has never been more crucial. One of the key issues at the heart of these concerns is the lack of transparency and control that users often have over their personal data.

AI systems are designed to continuously collect data to improve their performance, personalize user experiences, and make decisions based on insights derived from that data. This constant flow of information can include sensitive details about an individual's habits, preferences, and even emotional states. While AI can offer tailored experiences, it also places personal data at risk of misuse. For example, online platforms powered by AI often track users' browsing history, preferences, and interactions with content, compiling detailed user profiles. These profiles can be leveraged not just to improve service offerings but also to predict behaviours and influence decision-making, from purchasing choices to political opinions. The depth and scope of data collection can be alarming, especially when individuals are not fully aware of what is being collected or how it is being used. In many cases, the consent obtained from users is vague, buried in lengthy terms and conditions that are seldom read or understood, and often, users may not even be aware that they are consenting to such extensive data collection in the first place.

One of the most significant privacy risks is the potential for AI systems to breach user consent. AI-driven platforms may collect data without explicit, informed consent, often relying on users agreeing to broad terms of service or privacy policies that provide little transparency about data practices. In these situations, users may unknowingly give permission for their data to be shared with third parties or used for purposes that extend far beyond the initial scope of interaction. For example, when users sign up for an AI-powered app or service, they may unknowingly consent to the collection of more data than they realize, such as their location, purchasing habits, and interactions with other apps. Additionally, many AI systems rely on algorithms that evolve over time, meaning the data collection practices may change or expand without notifying the user. This lack of ongoing consent management increases the risk of privacy violations.

The issue of consent is further complicated by the fact that AI systems can often collect data in ways that users might not expect or fully understand. Some AI tools rely on passive data collection, meaning that the data is gathered automatically in the background without the user's active involvement or knowledge. For instance, mobile apps and websites powered by AI can track users' physical locations through GPS or monitor app usage patterns to gather information about their daily routines, health, or social interactions. While some of this data collection may be explicitly disclosed in terms of service agreements, the user may not have a clear understanding of the scope of data being collected or how that data is being used. AI systems can also gather and analyse data in ways that are difficult for users to comprehend. Machine learning algorithms can uncover hidden patterns or correlations within data, which may expose sensitive information about users that they did not intend to disclose. For example, AI may use data from a user's online behaviour to infer personal traits such as political affiliation, sexual orientation, or health conditions, potentially leading to unintended exposure of private information.

Another critical concern regarding AI-powered data collection is the issue of data security. The massive volume of personal data collected by AI systems makes it an attractive target for cyberattacks and data breaches. If not properly protected, this data can be accessed, stolen, or misused by malicious actors. A data breach involving AI-powered systems could expose sensitive personal information, such as credit card numbers, medical records, or even private communications. The consequences of such breaches can be devastating for users, leading to identity theft, financial loss, or even physical harm in extreme cases. As AI systems become more advanced, they also become more complex, increasing the challenge of securing the data they collect. Ensuring robust security protocols for AI-powered data systems is essential to mitigate these risks and protect users' privacy.

Moreover, there is also the issue of AI systems being used for surveillance purposes, raising concerns about mass data collection and its implications for personal freedoms. Governments and corporations may use AI to monitor individuals on a large scale, potentially infringing on privacy rights. AI-powered surveillance systems can track individuals' movements, analyse facial recognition data, and even listen to conversations, all without their explicit consent. While these technologies can be used to enhance security or improve public services, they also create opportunities for abuse, leading to concerns about mass surveillance, discrimination, and the erosion of civil liberties. The ability of AI systems to collect data in real-time and analyse it rapidly further intensifies the potential for misuse, as it enables entities to track individuals continuously and predict their behaviour based on past patterns. This creates the possibility of creating "digital profiles" that could influence personal decisions and even social interactions, all without the individual's explicit knowledge or consent.

Furthermore, the ethical considerations surrounding AI-driven data collection are complex. There is a fundamental question about the extent to which users should be able to control the data that is collected about them. In many instances, users are left with little choice but to accept the data collection practices of AI systems if they want to use the services offered by these platforms. This creates a power imbalance, with companies holding significant control over user data and individuals having limited ability to safeguard their privacy. Some AI systems are designed to offer benefits in exchange for access to personal data, such as personalized services or recommendations. However, the trade-off between the value of these services and the privacy risks they pose remains unclear, and in many cases, users may be unaware of the full extent of the trade-off they are making.

In response to these privacy risks, there have been growing calls for greater transparency, regulation, and control over AI-powered data collection. Many governments and organizations are pushing for stricter privacy regulations, such as the General Data Protection Regulation (GDPR) in the

European Union, which seeks to give users more control over their personal data. The GDPR, for example, mandates that organizations must obtain explicit consent from users before collecting their data and gives users the right to access, correct, and delete their data. However, while such regulations are a step in the right direction, they are not a panacea. The rapid pace of AI innovation and the global nature of digital platforms pose significant challenges to effective regulation. Additionally, not all countries have enacted comprehensive privacy laws, leaving many users vulnerable to data misuse. As AI technologies evolve, it will be crucial for policymakers to strike a balance between encouraging innovation and safeguarding user privacy.

In conclusion, AI-powered data collection poses significant risks to user privacy and consent. The ability of AI systems to gather and analyse vast amounts of personal data creates new opportunities for personalized services and automation, but it also exposes individuals to privacy violations, data breaches, and surveillance. The lack of transparency, the complexity of data collection methods, and the potential for misuse highlight the need for stronger privacy protections and more effective consent management. As AI continues to shape the future of technology, addressing these privacy risks will be essential to ensuring that individuals can maintain control over their personal data and safeguard their privacy in an increasingly digital world.

Potential for Harm: AI in military applications and autonomous systems poses risks if misused.

Ionized warfare, offering a new realm of possibilities, including increased operational efficiency, enhanced decision-making, and improved precision in targeting. However, this technological advancement also carries significant risks, especially when the AI systems are misused or fall into the wrong hands. The potential for harm from AI in military operations is considerable and multifaceted. These risks stem from various factors, including the complexity of AI systems, the lack of accountability in autonomous systems, and the difficulty in predicting how AI might behave in novel situations. The use of AI in warfare and military settings introduces unprecedented challenges for international security, ethical governance, and human rights, creating a pressing need to examine both the benefits and the dangers associated with these technologies.

One of the most significant concerns regarding AI in military applications is the possibility of unintended escalation. Autonomous weapons systems, designed to operate without human intervention, could make critical decisions on the battlefield based on algorithms that are not fully understood by their operators. These systems, depending on how they are programmed, could misinterpret situations or be unable to adapt to the complexities of real-world combat scenarios. A miscalculation or error in these systems could lead to unintended harm, including the loss of innocent lives, escalation of conflicts, or even triggering full-scale war due to a malfunction or erroneous interpretation of an adversary's actions. The lack of human oversight and the decision-making process being automated by AI could make it difficult for military personnel to assess the situation and intervene before harmful outcomes occur. This lack of accountability further complicates the scenario, as it may be challenging to attribute responsibility for miscalculations or acts of aggression carried out by AI-driven systems.

Moreover, the deployment of AI in military settings raises serious ethical and moral concerns, particularly in the context of warfare. Autonomous weapons systems could be used in a way that violates international humanitarian law, especially the Geneva Conventions, which protect civilian lives and property during armed conflicts. AI could potentially be programmed to make lethal decisions based solely on objective criteria, such as targeting military personnel or assets, without any consideration for the broader context, including the risk to civilian lives. The ability of AI to assess and act on its own could result in the indiscriminate use of force, undermining efforts to minimize collateral damage and protect non-combatants. This creates an ethical dilemma in which machines, devoid of human empathy, are making life-and-death decisions, raising questions about the morality of delegating such powers to algorithms that are not capable of nuanced judgment or understanding the consequences of their actions.

Another critical risk posed by AI in military applications is the potential for AI systems to be hacked or manipulated by adversarial forces. Military networks and autonomous systems are increasingly vulnerable to cyberattacks, and AI systems, given their complexity, could provide a new vector for cyber warfare. A successful hack of an AI-driven weapon or autonomous system could allow adversaries to take control of military assets, disable critical infrastructure, or manipulate the behaviour of automated systems to their advantage. Such cybersecurity vulnerabilities make it crucial for military organizations to implement robust safeguards to protect AI systems from external threats. If AI-driven systems are not adequately protected, they could be hijacked and used to cause widespread destruction, disrupt operations, or even create false flags that could escalate conflicts.

The rapid advancement of AI technology also brings concerns related to the arms race. Countries are racing to develop and deploy advanced AI-driven military systems, driven by the belief that possessing such technologies will provide a strategic advantage in warfare. This competitive drive could lead to the proliferation of autonomous weapons systems, increasing the risk of conflict. Furthermore, the widespread deployment of AI in military settings may lower the threshold for initiating military action. With autonomous weapons capable of acting without direct human control, countries may be more willing to engage in military operations or even act provocatively, believing that the AI systems will make more accurate and efficient decisions than human commanders. This could further destabilize international relations and increase the likelihood of military confrontations.

One of the greatest challenges posed by AI in military applications is the difficulty in ensuring that these systems operate within acceptable ethical boundaries and comply with international norms. AI systems are often designed with the assumption that they will function as intended, but they can behave unpredictably when confronted with novel or unexpected situations. The complexity of machine learning algorithms and the way they evolve based on data inputs creates an inherent challenge in ensuring that these systems remain under human control. Additionally, the lack of transparency in some AI systems, particularly those that employ deep learning techniques, makes it difficult to fully understand how decisions are made. This opacity in decision-making further complicates efforts to regulate and govern the use of AI in military applications. Ensuring that these systems operate ethically and do not cause undue harm will require comprehensive oversight and regulation, as well as the establishment of clear international frameworks that can guide the use of AI in warfare.

AI's potential for harm in military applications is also exacerbated by the lack of clear regulations governing its use in warfare. At present, there is a significant gap in international law regarding the use of autonomous weapons systems, leaving many countries to develop their own policies and standards. The absence of a global consensus on the rules surrounding AI in military settings means that countries can exploit these technologies without fear of legal repercussions. This lack of regulation makes it difficult to ensure that AI is used responsibly and in compliance with established ethical norms. The absence of a binding framework also means that the deployment of AI-driven military systems could vary significantly from one country to another, further increasing the risk of destabilization and conflict.

In conclusion, while the potential benefits of AI in military applications, such as increased precision, enhanced decision-making, and improved efficiency, are significant, the risks associated with these technologies cannot be ignored. The potential for harm from AI-driven autonomous systems in military operations is vast, ranging from unintended escalation and the violation of ethical principles to cybersecurity vulnerabilities and the risk of a global arms race. The deployment of AI in warfare introduces complex ethical, legal, and strategic challenges that require careful consideration and oversight. As AI continues to evolve and become more integrated into military applications, it is essential that international efforts focus on developing clear regulatory frameworks, ensuring transparency in AI decision-making, and holding nations accountable for the use of these technologies to prevent misuse and minimize the potential for harm. Without proper governance, the risks of AI in military applications could have devastating consequences, further complicating the already fragile state of global peace and security.

Chapter 4: The Ethical Dilemma

Balancing AI progress with ethical considerations

Balancing AI progress with ethical considerations is one of the most pressing challenges of the modern era. As artificial intelligence continues to evolve at an unprecedented rate, it brings with it a range of opportunities for innovation and societal advancement. From healthcare and education to transportation and entertainment, AI is poised to revolutionize virtually every aspect of life. However, alongside these advancements come significant ethical questions that need careful consideration. The balance between fostering AI progress and ensuring ethical standards can be complex, as rapid technological development often outpaces the development of corresponding ethical frameworks, laws, and regulations.

At the heart of the ethical considerations surrounding AI is the issue of accountability. As AI systems become more autonomous, questions arise regarding who is responsible when these systems cause harm or make decisions that negatively impact individuals or society. For instance, if an AI-powered self-driving car causes an accident, who should be held accountable—the car manufacturer, the software developer, or the AI itself? Similarly, in the case of AI-driven decision-making systems in sectors like hiring, lending, or law enforcement, biases present in the underlying algorithms can perpetuate and even amplify societal inequalities. Ensuring that AI systems are transparent, explainable, and accountable for their actions is vital to avoiding unintended consequences. This requires a commitment to integrating ethical principles such as fairness, justice, and human dignity into the development and deployment of AI technologies.

Another major ethical consideration in the development of AI is privacy. AI systems are designed to process vast amounts of data to learn and make decisions, but much of this data often involves personal and sensitive information. Without appropriate safeguards, AI systems can inadvertently infringe on individuals' privacy rights. For example, AI algorithms used for surveillance or predictive policing can infringe on citizens' privacy without their knowledge or consent. Similarly, AI tools used by corporations to analyse consumer behavior could lead to violations of personal privacy and autonomy. To ensure that AI does not erode privacy, it is crucial to implement strong data protection regulations, as well as promote ethical standards in data collection, storage, and use. These regulations should ensure transparency about how data is used and empower individuals to have greater control over their personal information.

AI also raises important concerns about fairness and inequality. Since AI systems are typically trained on large datasets, these datasets often reflect the biases and inequalities present in society. If not carefully managed, AI systems can perpetuate these biases, leading to discrimination in crucial areas such as hiring, criminal justice, and healthcare. For example, an AI system used in hiring could inadvertently Favor candidates of a certain race, gender, or socioeconomic background based on biased historical data. Similarly, AI algorithms used in the criminal justice system might disproportionately target certain communities, perpetuating existing racial or socioeconomic inequalities. To address these concerns, AI developers must ensure that their models are trained on diverse, representative datasets and are regularly audited for bias and fairness. They must also work closely with ethicists, social scientists, and affected communities to ensure that the deployment of AI technologies does not exacerbate societal divisions or reinforce systemic biases.

The issue of job displacement due to AI is another ethical challenge that must be addressed. As AI and automation technologies continue to improve, there is growing concern about the potential for widespread job loss in industries such as manufacturing, retail, and transportation. While AI has the potential to create new jobs and opportunities, the displacement of workers in certain sectors may result in increased inequality and economic instability. Ethical considerations in this area include not only ensuring fair transitions for displaced workers but also addressing broader societal implications. Governments and organizations must consider policies to promote reskilling and upskilling of the workforce, creating new roles that leverage the unique capabilities of humans and AI working together. Furthermore, there should be a commitment to developing AI systems that complement human labour rather than replace it, fostering a more inclusive economy that benefits all.

In addition to these concerns, the issue of AI's impact on democracy and decision-making cannot be overlooked. AI systems, particularly those used in the realm of social media, can influence public opinion, political campaigns, and even elections. Algorithms designed to recommend content can create echo chambers, amplify misinformation, and polarize societies. Moreover, AI-powered tools can be used to manipulate public opinion, as evidenced by the rise of deepfakes and other forms of AI-generated disinformation. As AI continues to play a role in shaping political discourse, it is crucial that ethical considerations are factored into the design and regulation of these systems. There must be safeguards in place to ensure that AI does not undermine democratic processes or contribute to the erosion of trust in institutions.

The ethical concerns surrounding AI progress also extend to global considerations. While the developed world may benefit from AI innovations, there is a risk that developing countries could be left behind. The unequal distribution of AI technologies could exacerbate existing global inequalities. Moreover, the development of AI technologies is often concentrated in a few powerful companies and countries, leading to concerns about monopolistic practices and the concentration of power. To address these issues, it is important to promote international cooperation and create global ethical frameworks for AI development that ensure the technology is used to benefit all of humanity, rather than being concentrated in the hands of a few.

As AI continues to evolve, it is imperative that ethical considerations are integrated into every stage of development, from research and design to deployment and regulation. This involves not only engaging ethicists and legal experts but also ensuring that the voices of diverse communities are heard. AI is a powerful tool, and when developed and used responsibly, it has the potential to drive significant positive change. However, without careful attention to the ethical implications of AI, the risks of harm—such as increased inequality, privacy violations, and the erosion of trust—are significant. To strike a balance between technological advancement and ethical responsibility, it is crucial that we remain committed to developing AI systems that prioritize human well-being, fairness, and accountability. This requires not only technological expertise but also a robust ethical framework that can guide decision-making in the age of AI.

The responsibility of developers and policymakers

The responsibility of developers and policymakers in today's rapidly advancing world is multifaceted and essential to ensuring that technological progress aligns with the broader goals of society. At the core of this responsibility lies the need for developers to produce technology that not only serves its intended purpose efficiently but also considers the potential impact it may have on various aspects of life—economic, social, and ethical. Likewise, policymakers play an equally crucial role in creating frameworks, regulations, and laws that govern the development and use of emerging technologies, ensuring that these advancements benefit the public while minimizing any harmful consequences. The relationship between developers and policymakers should, therefore, be collaborative, as it is the joint effort between these two entities that will ultimately shape the future of technology and its place in society.

One of the key responsibilities of developers is to design products, systems, and solutions that are secure, accessible, and user-friendly. This involves anticipating potential risks and taking steps to mitigate them through sound design practices, thorough testing, and continuous monitoring. With the increasing reliance on digital platforms and the growth of artificial intelligence, developers must be proactive in addressing issues such as privacy concerns, data security, and algorithmic biases. These considerations are particularly important as new technologies have the potential to influence various sectors, from healthcare to finance, education to transportation. Developers must act with an awareness of the broader implications their work can have on individuals, communities, and even entire countries. As technology becomes more embedded in daily life, the responsibility of ensuring that these innovations are ethical and serve the common good becomes more pronounced. Developers must also consider inclusivity in their designs, making sure that their products cater to diverse needs and ensure that marginalized groups are not excluded from benefiting from technological advancements.

Policymakers, on the other hand, have the critical task of establishing regulations and policies that ensure the responsible development and use of technology. Given the rapid pace at which technology evolves, it can be challenging for policymakers to keep up with innovations and their potential consequences. However, their role is indispensable in setting the legal and ethical standards for developers to follow.

Policymakers must strike a balance between fostering innovation and ensuring that emerging technologies are deployed responsibly. They need to address concerns related to privacy, intellectual property, consumer protection, and environmental sustainability, among others. For example, with the rise of AI, machine learning, and big data analytics, there is an urgent need for policymakers to introduce rules that prevent discriminatory practices and safeguard the rights of individuals. Furthermore, regulations surrounding cybersecurity, digital identity, and internet governance must be updated to reflect new threats and challenges posed by the ever-evolving technological landscape. Policymakers must also ensure that the benefits of technology are distributed fairly and equitably, taking steps to prevent monopolies or the concentration of power that could harm public welfare.

One significant area where the responsibility of developers and policymakers intersects is in the field of data privacy. With the explosion of personal data being collected, stored, and analysed by various organizations, it is critical that developers implement robust security measures to protect sensitive information. Developers must adopt best practices when it comes to data encryption, anonymization, and secure access protocols. But even the most advanced technological measures are ineffective if there is no overarching legal framework governing the use and sharing of data. This is where policymakers come into play, as they must establish laws and regulations that govern data usage and ensure that individuals' rights to privacy are protected. Governments and regulatory bodies across the world are increasingly recognizing the need for comprehensive data protection laws, such as the General Data Protection Regulation (GDPR) in Europe, which aims to give individuals greater control over their personal data. As new privacy challenges emerge, such as the use of biometric data and the spread of surveillance technologies, policymakers and developers must work together to ensure that new systems are transparent, accountable, and do not infringe upon individual rights.

Environmental sustainability is another area where developers and policymakers have overlapping responsibilities. Developers must consider the environmental impact of the technologies they create, particularly in sectors like energy, transportation, and manufacturing. The development of energy-efficient systems, the use of renewable energy sources, and the reduction of waste through circular economy models are all ways that developers can contribute to a greener future. On the other hand, policymakers must establish regulations that incentivize sustainable practices, create standards for environmental performance, and hold companies accountable for their ecological footprint. Through policies such as carbon pricing, emissions regulations, and the promotion of green technologies, governments can create the necessary conditions for developers to innovate in ways that support environmental goals. The transition to a low-carbon economy requires the collaboration of both developers, who are responsible for technological innovation, and policymakers, who can create the policy and regulatory environment that supports this shift.

In conclusion, the responsibilities of developers and policymakers are intertwined, and both groups must work collaboratively to ensure that technology serves the greater good. Developers must create solutions that are ethical, secure, inclusive, and environmentally sustainable, while policymakers must craft regulations that protect the public interest, promote fairness, and safeguard human rights. The rapid pace of technological advancement requires constant dialogue between these two groups to ensure that the development and deployment of new technologies do not outpace the ability of society to regulate them effectively. As technology continues to shape every aspect of modern life, the responsibility of developers and policymakers to act thoughtfully and responsibly has never been more critical. Only through a shared commitment to innovation and regulation can we create a future where technology enhances the quality of life for all and minimizes harm.

Regulation and governance of AI

Regulation and governance of Artificial Intelligence (AI) are crucial aspects of ensuring the ethical, safe, and responsible development and deployment of AI technologies. As AI becomes increasingly integrated into various sectors, from healthcare to finance, and from autonomous vehicles to military applications, the need for comprehensive frameworks governing its use has never been more apparent. The complexity of AI systems, their potential for both positive impact and unintended consequences, and the rapid pace at which these technologies are advancing necessitate a coordinated approach to regulation and governance. In this context, regulation refers to the creation of laws, rules, and guidelines to control the development and application of AI, while governance involves the broader, more strategic oversight, coordination, and accountability of AI at national and international levels.

The challenge of regulating AI is manifold. Firstly, the technology itself is multifaceted and dynamic, which makes it difficult to create rules that are sufficiently flexible to address the evolving nature of AI while also ensuring public safety and fairness. AI systems, particularly those driven by machine learning algorithms, can operate in ways that are opaque, making it difficult for humans to predict or understand their decisions. This "black-box" problem presents a challenge for regulators, who need to ensure that AI systems are transparent and accountable. Additionally, AI systems are often highly data-dependent, meaning that their effectiveness and fairness are heavily influenced by the quality and diversity of the data they are trained on. Bias in data can lead to biased AI outputs, raising concerns about fairness and discrimination, particularly in high-stakes areas like criminal justice, hiring, and lending.

To address these challenges, several countries and international organizations have proposed frameworks for the regulation and governance of AI. For example, the European Union has taken a leading role in AI regulation with its proposed Artificial Intelligence Act, which aims to create a risk-based framework for the regulation of AI. Under this act, AI systems are classified according to their level of risk, with stricter regulations applied to those deemed high-risk, such as AI used in critical infrastructure or decision-making in legal and healthcare settings. The act also includes provisions for transparency, accountability, and data governance, ensuring that AI systems can be audited and that individuals affected by

AI decisions have recourse for redress. The EU's approach is noteworthy because it emphasizes a precautionary principle, seeking to mitigate potential harm before it occurs rather than addressing problems reactively.

Similarly, other nations like the United States and China have made strides in AI governance, albeit with differing approaches. In the U.S., AI regulation has largely been decentralized, with various agencies, such as the Federal Trade Commission (FTC) and the National Institute of Standards and Technology (NIST), issuing guidelines and recommendations for AI development and deployment. However, unlike the EU, the U.S. does not have a comprehensive, overarching regulatory framework for AI, which has led to concerns about the lack of consistent standards and the potential for regulatory gaps. In contrast, China has taken a more centralized approach, with the government issuing sweeping guidelines for AI development and prioritizing AI as a critical national strategy. The Chinese approach places a heavy emphasis on control and surveillance, raising concerns about privacy and human rights in the context of AI deployment.

Beyond national frameworks, the governance of AI also involves international collaboration. Given the global nature of AI technologies, there is a growing recognition that international standards and agreements are necessary to ensure that AI is developed and used in ways that promote global good. The Organization for Economic Co-operation and Development (OECD) has been instrumental in fostering international cooperation on AI governance, promoting principles such as transparency, accountability, and human-centric AI. Similarly, the United Nations and other international bodies have called for global frameworks to address the ethical and societal implications of AI, particularly as it relates to human rights, equity, and environmental sustainability.

One of the key issues in AI regulation and governance is ensuring that AI systems are used ethically. Ethical considerations are central to AI governance because AI has the potential to profoundly impact people's lives, from how they are treated by automated systems to how their personal data is collected and used. Ethical frameworks for AI governance often include principles such as fairness, non-discrimination, transparency, accountability, and respect for privacy. For instance, the idea of "algorithmic fairness" seeks to ensure that AI systems do not disproportionately harm certain groups, particularly vulnerable populations. However, implementing fairness in AI is a complex task, as it involves addressing issues like data bias, the unintended consequences of algorithms, and the ethical implications of autonomous decision-making.

Another critical area of AI governance is ensuring that AI is developed and deployed in a way that respects privacy and protects personal data. As AI systems often rely on vast amounts of data to train and operate, data privacy concerns have become a focal point in regulatory discussions. The General Data Protection Regulation (GDPR) in the EU has set a high standard for data protection, and many experts believe that similar regulations should be adopted globally to ensure that individuals' privacy rights are protected in the context of AI. The challenge is that data used by AI systems is often personal and sensitive, and the deployment of AI in ways that respect privacy rights is a key concern for policymakers and civil society alike.

Accountability is another essential aspect of AI governance. As AI systems become more autonomous, it becomes increasingly difficult to pinpoint who is responsible when something goes wrong. If an AI system makes a harmful decision, such as denying someone a loan or misidentifying them in a security scan, who is to blame? Is it the developer who created the algorithm, the company that deployed it, or the AI itself? Legal frameworks need to be adapted to address these questions, ensuring that accountability mechanisms are in place for AI systems and that victims of AI-related harm have access to remedies.

The governance of AI also intersects with broader societal issues, including the future of work, economic inequality, and the concentration of power. As AI automates more tasks, there are concerns about job displacement and the potential for widening economic inequality. AI governance frameworks need to address these challenges by promoting policies that ensure a fair transition for workers affected by automation.

This may involve investing in reskilling and upskilling programs, creating new job opportunities in emerging AI sectors, and ensuring that the economic benefits of AI are widely distributed. Moreover, there is concern about the concentration of power in the hands of a few large technology companies that dominate the AI field. To prevent monopolistic practices and ensure that AI benefits society as a whole, there may be a need for stronger antitrust regulations and greater public oversight of AI research and development.

The regulation and governance of AI are also linked to broader geopolitical considerations. As AI technologies are increasingly seen as strategic assets, countries are competing to lead the AI race. This has led to concerns about an "AI arms race," with countries investing heavily in AI research and development for military and economic dominance. At the same time, AI's potential to be used for surveillance and control raises human rights concerns, particularly in authoritarian regimes. International governance frameworks for AI, therefore, must consider not only the technical and ethical dimensions of the technology but also its implications for global security, peace, and human rights.

In conclusion, the regulation and governance of AI are essential for ensuring that AI technologies are developed and deployed in a way that maximizes their benefits while minimizing risks. Given the complexity, potential risks, and rapid advancement of AI technologies, regulation must be proactive, flexible, and adaptive. Governance must be collaborative, involving stakeholders from government, industry, academia, and civil society. As AI continues to transform society, ensuring that it is governed by ethical principles, transparent practices, and accountability mechanisms will be crucial for fostering public trust and ensuring that AI serves the common good. The challenge is immense, but with careful planning, international cooperation, and a commitment to human values, it is possible to create a governance framework that ensures AI is used responsibly and for the benefit of all.

Chapter 5: AI in the Future

Predictions for AI's role in society

Artificial Intelligence (AI) is increasingly positioned as one of the most transformative forces in society, expected to reshape numerous facets of human life in the coming decades. Over the next 20 to 50 years, the role of AI is anticipated to expand significantly, affecting everything from labour markets and healthcare systems to education, entertainment, and even the very fabric of human interaction. As advancements in AI continue to accelerate, these technologies are predicted to profoundly impact society in ways both exciting and challenging. The convergence of AI with other emerging technologies like machine learning, robotics, quantum computing, and 5G networks is likely to drive rapid changes, setting the stage for a future that we are only beginning to understand.

First and foremost, one of the most pronounced areas where AI will play a crucial role is in the labour market. Automation, powered by AI, has already begun to replace routine and manual jobs, particularly in industries such as manufacturing, logistics, and customer service. Predictions indicate that this trend will continue, leading to further displacement of jobs that involve repetitive, predictable tasks. However, AI's potential to complement human capabilities rather than completely replace them suggests that the future of work will be characterized by more collaborative environments. Jobs that involve creative problem-solving, emotional intelligence, and complex decision-making—skills that AI currently struggles to emulate—will likely remain human-dominated. Furthermore, AI is expected to create entirely new industries and job categories that we cannot yet fully anticipate, much as the internet and computing did in the late 20th century. For example, the demand for AI specialists, data scientists, and machine ethics experts is expected to grow, creating a new class of high-skilled jobs that could help offset some of the employment losses in traditional sectors.

Despite these optimistic predictions, there is a significant concern surrounding AI's role in exacerbating economic inequality. As AI continues to automate more jobs, those who are unable to adapt or retrain may find themselves left behind. This could contribute to an increasing divide between highly educated, tech-savvy workers and those who are less equipped to navigate an AI-dominated world. The result could be a widening wealth gap, where the benefits of AI are disproportionately enjoyed by the wealthy and large corporations. Additionally, the concentration of AI technology in the hands of a few tech giants raises concerns about monopolistic power. If left unchecked, such concentration could undermine competition, reduce consumer choice, and diminish the overall societal benefits that AI could offer. Therefore, ensuring that AI development is inclusive and equitable will be a key challenge for policymakers in the years to come.

Another major area where AI is expected to have a profound impact is healthcare. AI-powered tools are already enhancing the diagnostic capabilities of doctors, improving treatment precision, and even assisting in the development of new drugs and therapies. Predictive algorithms, for instance, are being used to detect diseases like cancer in their earliest stages, potentially saving countless lives. Over the next few decades, AI could revolutionize healthcare by providing more personalized treatment options, monitoring patients in real time, and even performing complex surgeries with greater precision than human hands alone. One of the most exciting possibilities is the potential for AI to bridge the gap in healthcare access, especially in underserved or rural areas. AI systems could enable telemedicine, where patients consult with doctors remotely, and assist in diagnosing conditions in areas where healthcare professionals are scarce. Additionally, the rise of AI could lead to more efficient healthcare systems that reduce costs and improve outcomes, making quality healthcare accessible to a broader population.

However, the integration of AI into healthcare also raises a host of ethical issues that society must grapple with. One of the most pressing concerns is privacy—AI systems require vast amounts of personal data to function effectively, and this raises questions about who owns this data, how it is protected, and how it is used. The potential for AI systems to make life-altering decisions based on sensitive health information also presents ethical dilemmas related to accountability, bias, and transparency. For example, if an AI system incorrectly diagnoses a patient, determining who is responsible—whether it's the healthcare provider, the AI developer, or the system itself—could be a complex and contentious issue. Additionally, while AI can offer significant improvements in healthcare, there is also a risk that its widespread use could lead to an overreliance on technology, dehumanizing care, and undermining the role of human empathy in medical practice. As such, AI's integration into healthcare must be approached with caution, ensuring that the technology complements, rather than replaces, the human elements of care.

AI's influence will also extend to education, where it has the potential to radically transform teaching and learning methodologies. Personalized learning, powered by AI, could allow educators to tailor lessons to the individual needs of each student, helping to address disparities in educational attainment and learning styles. AI-driven tutoring systems are already being developed to provide students with real-time feedback, offering them targeted assistance in areas where they struggle the most. Furthermore, AI could help alleviate some of the administrative burdens on teachers, allowing them to focus more on pedagogy and less on grading, record-keeping, and other time-consuming tasks. The ability of AI to adapt and continuously improve based on student performance could lead to more effective educational practices, reducing the achievement gap between students of varying backgrounds.

However, there are concerns about the potential for AI to reinforce existing biases in educational systems. Algorithms are often trained on historical data, which may reflect societal inequalities, leading to systems that perpetuate discrimination. For example, AI systems used to assess student performance or allocate resources could inadvertently Favor certain demographic groups over others. Additionally, the reliance on AI in education could raise questions about privacy and the surveillance of students, as well as the potential for data to be used for purposes other than educational development. The challenge for educators and policymakers will be to ensure that AI is deployed in ways that enhance equity, fairness, and inclusivity, rather than deepening existing divides.

In addition to these practical applications, AI's role in entertainment and media is poised to evolve significantly. AI is already being used to create music, write stories, and generate art, pushing the boundaries of what constitutes creativity. It is expected that AI-driven tools will become increasingly sophisticated in generating content that rivals or even surpasses human-created works in terms of complexity, emotional depth, and aesthetic appeal. This could democratize creativity, enabling anyone with access to AI tools to produce high-quality art, music, or literature. On the other hand, this development may pose challenges for artists and creators whose livelihoods depend on traditional forms of content creation. The proliferation of AI-generated media also raises questions about the authenticity and value of human-created content. If AI systems can produce highly polished works of art, it could lead to a revaluation of what constitutes originality and creativity in the digital age.

Finally, AI's impact on human relationships and society's overall dynamics should not be underestimated. As AI becomes more integrated into our daily lives, it is likely to alter the way people interact with each other and the world around them. AI-powered virtual assistants, for instance, could serve as companions, and autonomous systems might replace human roles in customer service, caregiving, and even companionship. While these technologies could provide convenience and comfort, there is a risk that they may also contribute to social isolation, particularly among vulnerable populations like the elderly. The role of AI in social dynamics will require careful consideration, particularly as it pertains to emotional connections, trust, and the authenticity of human interactions. The growing use of AI in online spaces could also intensify issues like misinformation, manipulation, and privacy breaches, highlighting the need for robust safeguards and ethical frameworks to govern AI's role in society.

In conclusion, while AI promises remarkable advancements that could transform nearly every aspect of life, it is also clear that its future role in society will be fraught with challenges. Balancing innovation with ethical considerations, ensuring equity and access, and safeguarding human values in a technology-driven world will be crucial in determining whether AI fulfils its potential for the betterment of all. With thoughtful regulation, transparent development practices, and a focus on inclusivity, society can harness the benefits of AI while mitigating its risks, ensuring that this powerful technology serves humanity's best interests. The path forward is one of opportunity and responsibility, where the collaboration between humans and AI will define the trajectory of our shared future.

Possible solutions to mitigate AI risks

Artificial Intelligence (AI) has rapidly evolved, providing unprecedented opportunities across various industries. However, as AI systems become more integrated into daily life, the potential risks they pose, including ethical concerns, bias, job displacement, privacy violations, and even the threat of autonomous weapons, have become more pronounced. To address these risks and ensure the beneficial development of AI, a multifaceted approach is required, focusing on governance, transparency, regulation, ethical guidelines, and technological advances. Here, we outline several potential solutions that can help mitigate the risks associated with AI.

Establishing Robust Regulatory Frameworks

One of the most crucial steps in mitigating AI risks is the establishment of comprehensive and enforceable regulatory frameworks. Governments and international bodies must work together to create regulations that address not only the potential hazards AI poses but also the ethical considerations tied to its development and deployment. This would involve setting clear guidelines for the development, use, and monitoring of AI technologies, ensuring that they are aligned with human values and rights. These regulations could include standards for transparency, safety, and accountability, such as requiring AI systems to undergo audits and certifications before being deployed in critical sectors like healthcare, transportation, and finance.

Promoting Ethical AI Development

Ethical AI development is another key solution for mitigating AI risks. This involves ensuring that AI systems are designed and implemented in ways that align with ethical principles such as fairness, transparency, accountability, and non-discrimination. One approach to promoting ethical AI is the incorporation of diverse teams during the design phase of AI systems. A diverse team can help identify potential biases, ensuring that AI systems do not inadvertently reinforce harmful stereotypes or marginalize certain groups. Furthermore, ethical AI development involves prioritizing human oversight, where human operators can intervene in critical decisions made by AI systems, especially when these decisions affect people's lives and well-being.

Addressing Bias in AI Algorithms

AI systems can perpetuate and even exacerbate biases present in the data they are trained on. These biases can lead to unfair or discriminatory outcomes, particularly in areas such as hiring, lending, law enforcement, and healthcare. To mitigate this risk, one solution is to improve the data used to train AI models.

This includes ensuring that training data is diverse, representative, and free from inherent biases. Additionally, techniques like bias detection, algorithmic auditing, and continuous monitoring can help identify and rectify biased outputs during the AI lifecycle. Implementing fairness-aware algorithms is also a key strategy, where the AI model is designed to minimize the likelihood of biased decisions.

Ensuring Transparency and Explainability

The "black box" nature of many AI models is a significant challenge when it comes to accountability and trust. When AI systems make decisions that affect individuals or communities, it is crucial that these decisions can be understood and explained to the public. Ensuring AI transparency and explainability involves designing models that are interpretable, allowing users and stakeholders to understand the reasoning behind the AI's decisions. This can be achieved through advancements in explainable AI (XAI), which focuses on creating AI systems that can offer clear, understandable justifications for their outputs. Such transparency is essential for maintaining public trust and ensuring that AI decisions are made in accordance with legal, ethical, and societal standards.

Developing AI Safety Mechanisms

In certain high-risk applications, such as autonomous weapons, AI systems pose an existential risk if they are not properly designed and controlled. To mitigate these risks, AI safety mechanisms must be developed to ensure that AI behaves in predictable and controllable ways. This includes the use of failsafe mechanisms, such as kill switches or human override capabilities, which would allow humans to shut down or take control of AI systems in case they malfunction or act unexpectedly. Additionally, robust testing procedures must be in place to evaluate AI systems under a wide range of scenarios, ensuring they can handle unpredictable real-world conditions without causing harm.

Investing in Research for AI Alignment

AI alignment research focuses on ensuring that AI systems' goals and behaviours are aligned with human values and interests. This is particularly important for advanced AI, such as artificial general intelligence (AGI), which could surpass human intelligence and potentially act in ways that are not aligned with human well-being. AI alignment research aims to solve the problem of value specification—how to design AI systems that understand and pursue goals in a manner that is beneficial to humanity. Investing in this research will be crucial in preventing the development of AI systems that might act in ways that are harmful or contradictory to human intentions.

Promoting Public Awareness and Engagement

Public awareness and engagement are critical in ensuring that AI development is guided by the needs and interests of society as a whole. By fostering an informed public discourse around the potential risks and benefits of AI, individuals can contribute to the ongoing conversation about how AI should be developed and regulated. This includes raising awareness about the potential ethical implications of AI, encouraging public participation in decision-making processes, and ensuring that the development of AI is inclusive and democratic. Engaging with diverse stakeholders, including ethicists, policymakers, technologists, and ordinary citizens, can help shape AI development in ways that reflect a wide range of perspectives and values.

Global Cooperation and Standards

AI is a global phenomenon, and the risks associated with it do not respect national borders. As such, international cooperation and the establishment of global standards are essential for managing AI risks. Countries should work together to create shared guidelines and frameworks that govern the use of AI technologies, with an emphasis on promoting safety, security, and fairness. Global cooperation could involve sharing best practices, harmonizing regulations, and ensuring that AI development benefits all nations, not just the wealthiest ones. International treaties or agreements could also be considered to address the risks posed by military AI applications, ensuring that AI does not contribute to arms races or destabilize international security.

Lifelong Learning and Retraining Programs

One of the most immediate risks associated with AI is job displacement, as automation and AI technologies increasingly replace human labour in various industries. To mitigate this risk, governments and companies must invest in lifelong learning and retraining programs to help workers adapt to the changing job market. These programs should focus on equipping individuals with the skills needed to thrive in an AI-driven economy, such as digital literacy, data analysis, and machine learning. Furthermore, policies such as universal basic income (UBI) or wage subsidies could provide a safety net for individuals who are displaced by AI technologies.

Strengthening Cybersecurity Measures

AI systems are increasingly being integrated into critical infrastructure and services, making them attractive targets for cyberattacks. Malicious actors could exploit vulnerabilities in AI systems to cause harm, such as manipulating the behaviour of autonomous vehicles, hacking AI-powered healthcare systems, or even deploying AI in cyber warfare. To mitigate these risks, AI systems must be designed with robust cybersecurity measures in place. This includes using encryption, regular security audits, and developing AI-specific threat detection systems. Strengthening the security of AI systems will be essential in preventing malicious exploitation and ensuring that AI technologies remain safe and trustworthy.

Encouraging Ethical Investment in AI Development

Ethical investment in AI refers to prioritizing the funding and development of AI technologies that have a positive societal impact while minimizing harmful consequences. Investors, governments, and corporations should consider the ethical implications of the AI projects they fund, ensuring that these projects align with human rights and sustainability goals. By fostering a culture of responsible AI investment, the development of AI technologies can be steered toward applications that promote societal well-being, such as in healthcare, education, environmental protection, and public safety.

In conclusion, mitigating AI risks requires a holistic approach that combines regulation, ethics, transparency, research, and public engagement. By implementing these solutions, we can guide the development of AI technologies in a way that maximizes their benefits while minimizing their potential harms. Collaboration among governments, researchers, corporations, and the public will be crucial in creating a future where AI serves humanity's best interests and ensures the safety and prosperity of all people.

How Humans and AI Can Coexist Effectively

The rapid advancement of artificial intelligence (AI) has sparked discussions about how humans and AI can coexist effectively. While AI presents numerous benefits in various sectors, its integration into daily life raises concerns about ethical implications, workforce displacement, and societal changes. However, a balanced and collaborative approach can ensure that AI serves as an asset rather than a threat. By fostering human-AI collaboration, implementing ethical AI frameworks, enhancing education and workforce adaptation, ensuring transparency and accountability, and promoting inclusivity, society can maximize the benefits of AI while minimizing its challenges.

One of the most promising avenues for effective human-AI coexistence is collaboration rather than competition. AI is most effective when used as a tool to enhance human capabilities rather than replace them. For example, in healthcare, AI-powered diagnostic tools assist doctors in detecting diseases with higher accuracy and efficiency, allowing medical professionals to focus on patient care rather than spending excessive time analysing data. Similarly, in creative fields such as music and art, AI can generate ideas and assist artists in their creative process, leading to innovative works that blend human ingenuity with machine efficiency. By positioning AI as a complement to human effort, industries can leverage the strengths of both entities to achieve greater efficiency and innovation.

Implementing ethical AI frameworks is another crucial step in ensuring effective coexistence. AI development must be guided by ethical principles that prioritize fairness, transparency, and accountability. Governments, tech companies, and researchers must collaborate to establish regulations that prevent AI from being used for harmful purposes, such as biased decision-making or privacy violations. For instance, AI algorithms used in hiring processes should be audited to eliminate biases against certain demographic groups. Additionally, AI systems that make critical decisions, such as self-driving cars and financial trading algorithms, should be designed with clear ethical guidelines to ensure they align with human values. Establishing a strong ethical foundation for AI will help build public trust and mitigate potential risks associated with its widespread adoption.

Education and workforce adaptation play a vital role in preparing society for AI integration. As AI automates repetitive and mundane tasks, the workforce must adapt by developing new skills that align with the evolving job market. Governments and educational institutions should invest in programs that teach digital literacy, critical thinking, and problem-solving skills to prepare individuals for AI-driven workplaces. Encouraging lifelong learning through online courses and professional development programs can help workers stay relevant in an AI-enhanced economy. Additionally, businesses should focus on reskilling employees rather than replacing them, fostering a culture where human expertise and AI capabilities complement each other rather than compete.

Transparency and accountability are essential in fostering a healthy relationship between humans and AI. AI systems should be designed with explainability in mind, allowing users to understand how decisions are made. Black-box algorithms, which operate without clear explanations of their decision-making processes, can lead to mistrust and ethical concerns. By making AI more interpretable and holding developers accountable for its outcomes, society can ensure that AI operates within ethical boundaries. Moreover, establishing oversight bodies that monitor AI applications can help address concerns about misuse and unintended consequences. Providing the public with accessible information about AI's role in decision-making will enhance trust and encourage responsible usage.

Inclusivity is another critical factor in ensuring effective human-AI coexistence. AI should be developed with diverse perspectives in mind to avoid reinforcing biases and inequalities. Tech companies should involve diverse teams in AI development to ensure that algorithms are fair and representative of different communities. Additionally, AI applications should be designed to benefit all of society rather than only a privileged few. For example, AI-driven education tools can help bridge learning gaps for students in underserved communities, and AI-powered healthcare solutions can improve medical access in remote areas. By making AI development inclusive and equitable, society can ensure that its benefits are distributed fairly, leading to a more harmonious coexistence.

Ultimately, the key to effective human-AI coexistence lies in striking a balance between technological advancement and human values. Rather than fearing AI as a disruptive force, society should embrace it as a tool that enhances human potential. By fostering collaboration, implementing ethical guidelines, adapting the workforce, ensuring transparency, and promoting inclusivity, humans and AI can coexist in a way that maximizes benefits while minimizing risks. As AI continues to evolve, it is imperative to shape its development with thoughtful policies and ethical considerations to create a future where both humans and AI thrive together.

Conclusion

AI is neither inherently good nor bad—it is a tool shaped by how it is developed and used. While its benefits can revolutionize industries and improve lives, its drawbacks must be addressed to ensure a fair and ethical future. The key lies in responsible innovation and strategic policymaking.

Chapter 6: AI and Creativity

The impact of AI on art, music, and literature

Artificial intelligence has profoundly transformed the realms of art, music, and literature, introducing new possibilities while simultaneously challenging traditional notions of creativity, originality, and authorship. In the visual arts, AI-driven programs such as DeepDream, DALL·E, and Midjourney have demonstrated the ability to generate breathtakingly intricate images, either by mimicking the styles of historical painters like Van Gogh, Picasso, and Monet or by producing entirely new and surreal compositions that challenge human perceptions of artistic expression. These AI models, trained on vast datasets of classical and contemporary artworks, have blurred the line between human-made and machine-generated creativity, raising important philosophical and ethical questions about whether art's value is derived from the process of creation or the final product itself. While some critics argue that AI-generated art lacks the depth of human emotion and intentionality, others see it as an innovative tool that expands artistic possibilities, allowing both professional artists and amateurs to experiment with styles, textures, and techniques that might otherwise take years to master. The rise of AI-generated art has also disrupted traditional art markets, as digital artworks created by machines have sold for thousands, even millions, of dollars at prestigious auction houses, sparking debates about authorship, intellectual property, and the future of creative industries.

Similarly, in the world of music, artificial intelligence has made groundbreaking strides, with machine learning algorithms capable of composing original symphonies, generating dynamic soundscapes, and even mimicking the distinct styles of legendary musicians. Platforms like AIVA, OpenAI's MuseNet, and Google's Magenta have demonstrated that AI can analyse vast amounts of musical compositions, understand patterns and structures, and then create melodies and harmonies that evoke deep emotional responses, sometimes rivalling compositions created by human musicians. AI-generated music has already been used in film scores, video game soundtracks, and commercial jingles, leading to speculation about whether the role of human composers will diminish over time or whether AI will simply serve as a powerful tool to aid musical innovation. Some musicians view AI as a collaborator, capable of providing inspiration, suggesting chord progressions, or even generating entire instrumental arrangements that they can refine and personalize, while others worry that automated composition tools could lead to a homogenization of music, where formulaic AI-generated songs flood the industry and diminish the appreciation for human craftsmanship. Moreover, AI-powered voice synthesis technology has made it possible to recreate the voices of deceased artists, raising ethical concerns about posthumous performances and the boundaries of artistic legacy.

In literature, AI's influence has been equally disruptive, as natural language processing (NLP) models such as OpenAI's GPT series and Google's BERT have demonstrated remarkable proficiency in generating human-like text, ranging from poetry and short stories to full-length novels, screenplays, and journalistic articles. These AI systems, trained on massive datasets of books, essays, and historical texts, can craft narratives with coherent plots, well-developed characters, and stylistic flourishes that closely resemble those of human authors. While AI-generated literature has impressed many with its ability to mimic the works of famous writers and even create original, thought-provoking content, it has also sparked debates about authenticity, intellectual property, and the implications of machines producing creative works. Publishers and literary critics question whether AI-generated books should be considered genuine literature or merely sophisticated simulations of human storytelling, and concerns have emerged regarding the potential for AI-written misinformation, the devaluation of human authorship, and the broader consequences for the publishing industry. However, some authors and poets embrace AI as a tool for overcoming writer's block, brainstorming new ideas, or co-writing experimental pieces, viewing it not as a replacement for human creativity but as an augmentation of it. The rise of AI-written literature has also democratized the writing process, allowing those without formal literary training to generate compelling narratives, which, while empowering, also raises concerns about oversaturation in the market and the erosion of traditional literary craftsmanship.

Beyond the creative process itself, AI's impact on art, music, and literature extends to the way audiences engage with and consume creative works. Recommendation algorithms, powered by machine learning, now shape how people discover new books, songs, and artworks, influencing cultural trends and reinforcing personalized artistic experiences. Streaming services like Spotify, Netflix, and YouTube use AI to curate content based on users' preferences, leading to highly individualized consumption patterns but also raising concerns about the narrowing of cultural exposure, as people are increasingly shown what aligns with their past preferences rather than being encouraged to explore unfamiliar genres or styles. Additionally, AI-powered tools are being used to analyse audience reactions, predict trends, and even optimize creative content for maximum engagement, which has led to a shift in how art, music, and literature are produced, with some creators tailoring their works to align with algorithmic preferences rather than purely artistic intent.

Despite these transformative advancements, the integration of AI into creative fields has sparked broader philosophical and ethical debates about the nature of creativity itself. Is creativity defined solely by human emotion, lived experience, and intentionality, or can machines—trained on vast amounts of human-generated data—develop their own form of artistic intuition? As AI-generated works become more sophisticated, will society continue to value human creativity in the same way, or will the distinction between human and machine-created art become increasingly irrelevant? Furthermore, legal and ethical questions surrounding ownership and copyright remain unresolved, as existing intellectual property laws struggle to address the complexities of AI-generated content. If an AI program creates a best-selling novel or a chart-topping song, who owns the rights—the programmer, the user who provided the input, or the AI itself? The lack of clear legal frameworks has already led to disputes, with some arguing for AI-generated works to be classified as public domain while others advocate for new legal definitions that recognize AI as a tool rather than a creator.

Ultimately, artificial intelligence is redefining the boundaries of artistic, musical, and literary expression, not by replacing human creativity, but by expanding its possibilities, challenging conventional ideas about authorship, and reshaping the ways in which creative content is produced, distributed, and consumed. While some view these advancements with apprehension, fearing the loss of traditional craftsmanship and the commodification of creativity, others see AI as a powerful ally that democratizes artistic expression, enables new forms of collaboration, and pushes the limits of human imagination. As AI continues to evolve, the intersection of technology and creativity will remain a dynamic and controversial space, forcing society to continuously reexamine what it means to be an artist, a musician, or a writer in an era where machines are no longer just tools but active participants in the creative process.

Can AI be truly creative?

The question of whether artificial intelligence (AI) can truly be creative is a complex and multifaceted one. At its core, creativity is often associated with the ability to generate new, original ideas that are not just functional but also imaginative, inspiring, and meaningful. When humans engage in creative endeavours, they draw upon a combination of experience, intuition, emotion, and cognitive processes to come up with something novel. This process seems inherently tied to the human condition—our capacity for self-reflection, our emotions, and our ability to navigate the nuances of personal and collective experiences. Yet, as AI systems become more advanced, their capacity to produce content that appears creative has raised questions about whether these machines can indeed match or even surpass human creativity. In order to explore this question thoroughly, it is important to look at both the current capabilities of AI in creative fields and the philosophical implications of creativity itself.

One of the most prominent areas in which AI's creative abilities are explored is in the realm of the arts. In recent years, AI has demonstrated the ability to compose music, generate visual art, write poetry, and even produce works of fiction. Programs like OpenAI's GPT-3 and Google's DeepDream have become capable of generating text that mimics the nuances of human language and producing images that evoke the same kind of abstract thought as traditional artwork. Music composition tools like Aiva and Amper have even produced symphonies, while AI-generated art has been showcased in galleries, sparking debates about the authenticity and meaning behind such works. However, while these outputs may seem impressive, there is an ongoing debate about whether these creations can be considered truly creative. Critics argue that AI lacks the intentionality, consciousness, and emotional depth that characterize human creativity. They contend that AI-generated art is essentially a recombination of existing data, algorithms, and patterns rather than a true expression of original thought.

On the other hand, proponents of AI creativity argue that creativity is not necessarily tied to human consciousness or intentionality. In this view, creativity is a process of pattern recognition, problem-solving, and innovation, all of which AI systems are quite capable of performing. AI's ability to analyse vast amounts of data, recognize patterns, and generate new combinations of ideas can be seen as a form of creative exploration. For example, AI systems can sift through thousands of years of music history to identify trends, structures, and harmonies, and then apply these insights to create novel compositions. Similarly, AI tools can analyse large datasets of visual art, identifying the styles, techniques, and motifs used by various artists across time. With this knowledge, they can create new works that push the boundaries of traditional artistic forms. In this sense, AI can be seen as a collaborator in the creative process, offering new perspectives and possibilities that might not have been considered by human creators.

Yet, even in this collaborative view, questions persist about the authenticity of AI's creativity. Some critics argue that creativity is not simply about producing novel or innovative outputs but also about understanding the context in which these creations are made. Human creativity, in this sense, is deeply tied to culture, history, emotion, and the experience of being human. A painting or a symphony is not merely a collection of shapes, colours, or sounds; it is an expression of the artist's worldview, struggles, and aspirations. AI, in contrast, lacks the ability to experience the world in this way. It does not have a sense of self, nor does it experience emotions or have the same subjective understanding of the world that a human artist does. This lack of lived experience raises the question: can AI really be said to create in the same sense that humans do? Or is it simply producing outputs based on the patterns it has been trained to recognize, devoid of any true emotional or personal connection?

Philosophically speaking, the question of AI's creativity also touches on broader issues about the nature of creativity itself. Is creativity a purely human trait, or can it be replicated by machines? Some philosophers argue that creativity is an inherently human endeavour, one that is tied to our ability to reflect on our existence and our place in the world. This view holds that the creative process involves more than just the generation of new ideas; it also requires a certain level of self-awareness, intentionality, and emotional engagement with the world. AI, by contrast, operates based on predefined algorithms and data sets. It does not "think" in the same way humans do. While it can generate new ideas or combinations, these ideas are always the product of its programming and the data it has been trained on, rather than a product of genuine insight or self-expression. In this sense, AI could be seen as merely a tool for creating, rather than a true creative agent.

Alternatively, others argue that creativity is not inherently tied to consciousness or emotion but can be viewed as a function of problem-solving and innovation. In this view, creativity is the ability to generate solutions to complex problems, make connections between disparate ideas, and think outside the box. From this perspective, AI's ability to perform these tasks with speed and precision could be seen as evidence of its creative potential. After all, AI systems are capable of producing works of art that are both novel and aesthetically pleasing, even if they do not have the emotional depth or intentionality that human creators might bring to the table. This raises a broader question about the role of emotion and intent in creativity: do these factors truly define creativity, or are they simply a byproduct of the human experience that is not essential to the creative process itself?

Moreover, the role of the human creator in the age of AI also complicates the definition of creativity. In many cases, AI is not working in isolation but rather alongside human creators, augmenting their capabilities and expanding the possibilities of creative expression. For example, AI can be used to generate musical compositions, but it is still up to the human composer to decide how those compositions will be used, performed, and integrated into a larger work. Similarly, AI-generated art may serve as a starting point for human artists to explore new ideas and directions in their own work. In this sense, AI can be seen as a tool that enhances human creativity, offering new ways to think about and engage with the creative process. Rather than replacing human creativity, AI might be better understood as a partner in a broader collaborative effort, one in which human and machine work together to push the boundaries of what is possible.

In conclusion, the question of whether AI can truly be creative does not have a simple answer. It depends on how we define creativity and what we believe constitutes the essence of creative expression. If creativity is defined as the ability to generate new and original ideas, then AI can certainly be seen as creative, especially when it comes to its ability to generate novel compositions, works of art, and other forms of expression. However, if creativity is viewed as something that is inherently tied to human experience, emotion, and intentionality, then AI's output might be seen as lacking the depth and authenticity of human creativity. Ultimately, AI's role in the creative process may be best understood not as a replacement for human creators, but as a powerful tool that can augment and expand our creative possibilities. In this collaborative framework, AI's creative potential becomes a question of how it can assist humans in exploring new avenues of creativity, rather than whether it can create in the same way that humans do

Ethical concerns in AI-generated content

As artificial intelligence (AI) continues to evolve and expand into various industries, one of its most influential developments has been in the realm of content creation. From writing articles to generating visual art, AI-generated content is increasingly becoming a significant part of modern media and culture. However, this advancement has raised numerous ethical concerns that must be addressed as AI becomes more integrated into society. These ethical concerns touch upon issues of authorship, bias, misinformation, copyright infringement, and the impact on human creativity. As AI technologies improve, the potential for misuse grows, making it imperative to have a dialogue about the moral and social implications of this new frontier. This essay explores the key ethical concerns surrounding AI-generated content, with a focus on how these challenges may impact individuals, industries, and society as a whole.

One of the primary ethical concerns with AI-generated content is the issue of authorship and originality. Traditional notions of authorship, particularly in fields like literature, art, and journalism, have long been grounded in the idea that human creators are the originators of their work. However, when AI systems generate content, the question arises as to who should be considered the "author." Is it the programmer who created the algorithm, the AI system itself, or the individual who commissions the content? This question becomes even more complex in cases where the AI uses existing content as training data. For example, if an AI system is trained on a vast array of copyrighted texts to generate a new piece of writing, does that new work still belong to the AI, or does the responsibility fall on the creators of the training data? In some cases, AI-generated content may be indistinguishable from human-created content, leading to challenges in determining whether proper attribution has been given to the original creators. This dilemma raises important questions about intellectual property rights and the ownership of content in the age of artificial intelligence.

Another significant ethical issue is the potential for AI-generated content to perpetuate or amplify biases. Machine learning algorithms, which underpin many AI systems, learn from large datasets that may contain historical biases or prejudices. If the training data reflects biased or discriminatory practices, the AI model is likely to replicate these biases in its generated content. For instance, an AI system trained on biased news articles or social media posts might create content that reinforces harmful stereotypes or misinformation about specific groups of people. This is particularly concerning in areas such as journalism and social media, where biased content can influence public opinion, reinforce harmful stereotypes, and perpetuate inequality. For example, AI-generated news articles may be more likely to reflect the biases of the data they were trained on, resulting in inaccurate or misleading information that can sway public perception. Ensuring that AI systems are trained on diverse, unbiased datasets is essential to mitigate the risks of perpetuating harmful biases.

The potential for AI-generated content to spread misinformation is another critical ethical concern. In an era where fake news and misinformation can spread rapidly through social media and other online platforms, the ability of AI to generate realistic-looking content has raised alarms. AI systems can create highly convincing fake news articles, videos, and social media posts that can mislead audiences into believing false information. For example, deepfake technology can be used to create realistic videos in which people appear to say or do things they never actually did, causing reputational harm and manipulating public opinion. The ability to generate highly persuasive but entirely fabricated content poses significant risks to public trust, especially in areas like politics and public health. AI-generated misinformation can be used to interfere with elections, incite violence, or promote harmful conspiracy theories. Addressing this challenge requires the development of tools to detect and combat AI-generated misinformation, as well as greater transparency in how AI systems are used to generate content.

In addition to the risks posed by misinformation, there are concerns about the ethical implications of AI-generated content in the context of copyright infringement. As AI systems increasingly generate content, it becomes more difficult to determine whether the work is original or a derivative of existing works. Many AI systems are trained on large datasets that include copyrighted materials, and the content generated by these systems may unintentionally infringe upon the intellectual property rights of creators. For example, an AI-generated image may closely resemble an artwork created by a human artist, raising questions about whether the AI system has violated copyright laws. This issue is particularly relevant as AI-generated content becomes more widely used in creative industries like music, visual art, and literature. In some cases, creators may feel that their work is being exploited without proper compensation or recognition, leading to calls for clearer guidelines around AI and copyright. Determining the legal and ethical boundaries of AI-generated content in relation to copyright law will require collaboration between lawmakers, content creators, and technology developers.

The impact of AI-generated content on human creativity is also an important ethical consideration. While AI has the potential to enhance creativity by providing new tools for artists and writers, there are concerns that it could diminish the value of human creativity. As AI systems become more capable of generating high-quality content, there is a fear that human creators may be sidelined in Favor of machines. This could result in a shift in the nature of creative work, with AI systems taking over tasks traditionally performed by humans, such as writing, painting, or composing music. While AI can undoubtedly serve as a valuable tool for human creators, there is a risk that it could replace the unique and personal touch that human creators bring to their work. This raises questions about the role of AI in creative industries and whether the proliferation of AI-generated content could devalue human artistic expression. Additionally, the rise of AI-generated content may lead to job displacement for individuals working in fields like journalism, content writing, and graphic design. The ethical implications of AI on employment and human creativity must be carefully considered as AI continues to evolve.

Finally, the broader societal impact of AI-generated content raises ethical questions related to the potential for manipulation and control. As AI-generated content becomes more widespread, there is the risk that it could be used to manipulate public opinion or advance particular political or ideological agendas. For instance, AI could be employed to create propaganda or influence elections by generating persuasive but misleading content that sways voters. Additionally, large tech companies or governments could use AI to create content that shapes public perception in ways that benefit their interests. The ability to generate personalized, targeted content at scale could give those in power unprecedented control over public discourse. This raises important ethical concerns about the concentration of power in the hands of a few entities that control AI technologies. It is essential to establish regulatory frameworks that ensure AI-generated content is used responsibly and ethically, protecting individuals from manipulation and ensuring that the technology serves the public good.

In conclusion, while AI-generated content holds tremendous potential for innovation and creativity, it also presents a wide range of ethical concerns that must be addressed. Issues related to authorship, bias, misinformation, copyright infringement, and the impact on human creativity are at the forefront of this ongoing debate. As AI continues to advance, it is crucial to establish ethical guidelines and regulatory frameworks that promote responsible use of the technology and mitigate the risks it poses. Collaboration between technology developers, policymakers, content creators, and the public will be essential in ensuring that AI-generated content is used in ways that benefit society while minimizing harm. The ethical challenges associated with AI-generated content are complex, but with careful consideration and proactive action, it is possible to navigate these challenges and create a future where AI enhances rather than undermines human creativity and societal well-being.

Chapter 7: AI and Human Interaction

AI and Human Interaction

Artificial Intelligence (AI) is increasingly influencing various facets of our lives, and its role in human interaction is at the centre of contemporary technological discussions. Chapter 7 focuses on understanding how AI systems interact with humans, shaping communication, collaboration, and the nature of work. Human interaction with AI spans a wide spectrum of applications, from personal assistants like Siri and Alexa to more complex AI systems designed to augment professional roles in healthcare, education, and business. The chapter provides a comprehensive overview of how these interactions are not only transforming user experiences but also raising critical questions about the future of human relationships with technology. With AI now able to understand natural language, recognize emotions, and even anticipate user needs, the line between human-like interaction and machine efficiency is becoming increasingly blurred.

The chapter opens by discussing the fundamental changes in communication brought about by AI. In the past, humans have had to adapt to the limitations of machines, operating within rigid interfaces and predefined commands. However, AI has shifted this dynamic by enabling natural language processing (NLP) capabilities, allowing users to communicate with machines in a more intuitive and human-like manner. The development of NLP technologies has allowed AI systems to interpret spoken language with remarkable accuracy, enabling conversational interactions that mimic those between humans. Whether it's a chatbot helping a customer with technical support or an AI assistant scheduling appointments, these systems have bridged the gap between human communication and machine responses. As a result, interactions with AI feel increasingly fluid and seamless, which has been integral to the widespread adoption of virtual assistants and customer service AI.

AI's ability to comprehend and replicate human emotional responses is another significant aspect of its interaction with humans. Chapter 7 delves into how AI systems, equipped with sentiment analysis and emotion recognition, are now able to gauge and respond to human feelings in real time. Whether it is through text analysis, voice tone interpretation, or facial expression recognition, AI is learning to recognize emotions and adjust its responses accordingly. For example, in therapeutic settings, AI-driven applications can detect signs of distress or sadness and provide empathetic responses to users. In educational contexts, AI systems can personalize learning experiences based on the emotional state of students, adapting teaching methods to increase engagement. However, this raises ethical concerns about the manipulation of emotions and the potential for AI to become too persuasive or invasive, leading to questions about how much influence machines should have over human emotional states.

Another central theme in this chapter is the impact of AI on collaboration between humans and machines in the workplace. The nature of work is undergoing a profound transformation, with AI systems not only automating repetitive tasks but also collaborating with human workers on more complex projects. In industries such as manufacturing, healthcare, and finance, AI-powered tools are assisting professionals by analysing large datasets, identifying patterns, and providing insights that would otherwise be time-consuming for humans to uncover. This symbiotic relationship between humans and AI has led to greater efficiency, innovation, and accuracy. However, the chapter also highlights the challenges that arise when AI systems replace jobs traditionally performed by humans. As machines take over tasks, workers must adapt by acquiring new skills, which leads to questions about job displacement and the evolving nature of labour markets.

One of the key insights in this chapter is the ethical implications of AI-human interaction. The increasing complexity and autonomy of AI systems raise concerns about their role in decision-making processes. For instance, in criminal justice, AI tools are being used to assess recidivism risks and make sentencing recommendations. While these systems aim to improve objectivity and reduce human biases, there is growing concern about the transparency of AI decision-making. How can humans trust AI when its decision-making processes are often opaque and not fully understood? Furthermore, there is a fear that the data used to train AI models can perpetuate existing biases, leading to discriminatory outcomes. As AI continues to influence areas such as hiring, law enforcement, and finance, ensuring fairness, accountability, and transparency in human-AI interactions will become a central issue in the development of future AI systems.

Finally, the chapter concludes by looking ahead at the future of AI and human interaction. It emphasizes the need for ongoing research and development to create AI systems that are not only effective but also ethically sound. One of the most exciting prospects is the potential for AI to serve as a tool for enhancing human capabilities rather than replacing them. By focusing on collaboration rather than competition, AI can be designed to complement human intelligence and creativity, leading to new forms of innovation and problem-solving. However, the future also presents significant challenges, particularly in ensuring that AI systems are aligned with human values and that their integration into society does not exacerbate existing inequalities. As AI continues to evolve, the relationship between humans and machines will be shaped by both technological advancements and the ethical frameworks that guide their use. The chapter urges readers to think critically about the ways in which AI interacts with humanity, encouraging ongoing dialogue about the implications of this technology for future generations.

AI in customer service and social interactions

Artificial intelligence (AI) has revolutionized the landscape of customer service and social interactions, transforming how businesses engage with their customers and how people communicate with each other in the digital age. At the core of this transformation lies AI's ability to streamline processes, improve efficiency, and provide personalized experiences, reshaping customer service into a more accessible and responsive domain. The emergence of AI technologies, such as chatbots, virtual assistants, and predictive analytics, has led to a paradigm shift where businesses can offer immediate, around-the-clock service, overcoming traditional barriers like time zones and resource constraints. AI systems can handle a vast array of customer inquiries, often providing quick and accurate responses, which reduces wait times and enhances customer satisfaction. By automating routine tasks, AI also allows human agents to focus on more complex and nuanced issues, leading to an overall more effective service model.

One of the primary ways AI has impacted customer service is through the use of chatbots and virtual assistants. These AI-driven tools are designed to simulate human conversation and are commonly deployed across various platforms, from websites to mobile apps. Chatbots can handle a wide range of inquiries, from basic FAQs to more specific requests, and they can learn from past interactions to improve their responses over time. This constant learning and adaptation, driven by machine learning algorithms, allows AI to offer increasingly relevant solutions. For example, when a customer asks about a product's availability or delivery times, the chatbot can provide real-time data, making the interaction seamless and efficient. Moreover, chatbots are available 24/7, providing customers with the flexibility to engage at their convenience, whether it's late at night or early in the morning. This continuous availability increases customer engagement and satisfaction, as customers do not have to wait for business hours to resolve their issues.

In addition to providing direct support through chatbots, AI is also used to analyse vast amounts of data and generate insights that can improve the overall customer experience. By leveraging predictive analytics, AI systems can anticipate customer needs and proactively offer solutions. For instance, if a customer has previously ordered a product or service, AI can recommend similar items or follow-up services based on past behaviour. This ability to predict what a customer might need or want next adds a level of personalization to interactions that was previously difficult to achieve on a large scale. It also allows businesses to tailor their marketing strategies and communication to individual customers, creating a more engaging and relevant experience. AI systems can track customer behaviour across multiple channels, including social media, websites, and email communications, to gain a holistic understanding of their preferences and interests. With this information, businesses can engage customers in a more targeted and effective way, ultimately fostering stronger relationships and increasing customer loyalty.

While AI has made significant strides in enhancing customer service, its role in social interactions extends beyond business contexts. In personal communications, AI-powered platforms have facilitated new forms of interaction and connectedness. Social media networks, messaging apps, and even dating apps have incorporated AI to improve user experiences and make social interactions more engaging. For example, AI algorithms are used in platforms like Facebook, Instagram, and Twitter to curate personalized feeds for users, showing them content that aligns with their interests and preferences. This level of customization creates a more engaging experience for users, as they are more likely to interact with content that resonates with them.

Similarly, dating apps like Tinder and Bumble use AI to match users based on their preferences, behaviours, and even past interactions, increasing the chances of a successful match and fostering meaningful connections.

Another important area where AI plays a role in social interactions is in the realm of accessibility. AI-powered technologies such as speech recognition, real-time translation, and text-to-speech tools have made it easier for individuals with disabilities to communicate and engage with others. For example, AI-driven speech recognition systems can transcribe spoken words into text, allowing individuals with hearing impairments to participate in conversations more easily. Similarly, real-time translation services powered by AI enable people who speak different languages to communicate effectively without the need for human translators. These advancements have had a profound impact on social interactions, breaking down barriers of communication and enabling greater inclusivity in both personal and professional settings.

However, while AI's role in customer service and social interactions has brought about numerous benefits, there are also challenges and concerns that need to be addressed. One of the most significant concerns is the potential loss of human touch in customer service. Although AI can handle many tasks with efficiency, it lacks the emotional intelligence and empathy that human agents bring to interactions. For complex or sensitive issues, customers may prefer to speak with a human representative who can provide a more personalized and empathetic response. Additionally, over-reliance on AI may lead to frustration if customers are unable to resolve their issues through automated channels and feel that they are being dismissed or ignored. Striking the right balance between AI-driven automation and human intervention is essential to ensuring that customer service remains effective and compassionate.

In social interactions, AI also raises concerns related to privacy and data security. Many AI-powered platforms rely on collecting and analysing vast amounts of personal data in order to provide personalized recommendations and experiences. This data collection can raise concerns about how personal information is stored, shared, and used, particularly when it comes to sensitive data such as location, browsing habits, or communication preferences. There is also the issue of algorithmic bias, where AI systems may inadvertently perpetuate stereotypes or Favor certain groups over others due to biased data or programming. This can lead to discriminatory outcomes, whether in the context of customer service or social interactions. To mitigate these risks, it is crucial for businesses and developers to implement strong data protection measures, ensure transparency in how AI systems make decisions, and regularly audit algorithms to detect and correct any biases.

The future of AI in customer service and social interactions is poised to evolve even further as technology advances. In the coming years, we can expect AI to become even more integrated into the fabric of daily life, with greater capabilities for understanding and responding to human emotions, preferences, and intentions. For example, future AI systems may be able to detect subtle changes in a customer's tone of voice or facial expression and adjust their responses, accordingly, making interactions more human-like. Furthermore, as AI becomes more sophisticated, it may be able to engage in more natural, fluid conversations with users, moving beyond scripted responses to offer more dynamic and contextually relevant interactions.

At the same time, businesses will continue to explore ways to enhance customer service through the use of AI-powered tools. From voice assistants like Amazon's Alexa and Apple's Siri to more advanced chatbots capable of conducting full conversations, AI will continue to play a central role in providing faster and more efficient service. AI's ability to handle large volumes of customer interactions simultaneously will be particularly valuable in industries such as e-commerce, telecommunications, and banking, where customer inquiries can be both frequent and varied. Additionally, the growing use of AI in social interactions will continue to reshape how people communicate and connect with one another. AI-powered virtual assistants will become more integrated into social media platforms, helping users manage their online presence, schedule events, and even engage in real-time conversations with friends and family.

In conclusion, the integration of AI into customer service and social interactions has led to a profound shift in how businesses and individuals communicate. AI has enhanced customer service by providing faster, more efficient, and personalized experiences, while also offering new avenues for social engagement. However, as AI becomes increasingly prevalent, it is essential to address concerns related to privacy, data security, and the potential loss of human touch in interactions. By striking the right balance between automation and human interaction, AI has the potential to improve both customer service and social communication, making our interactions more seamless, inclusive, and meaningful.

Chatbots, virtual assistants, and emotional AI

Chatbots, virtual assistants, and emotional AI are cutting-edge technologies that have revolutionized the way we interact with machines and perform daily tasks. These technologies, while distinct in some aspects, share underlying principles of artificial intelligence (AI) that enable them to simulate human-like interaction and enhance user experience. The journey of chatbots began with the development of simple text-based interfaces, which were designed to respond to specific commands or answer basic questions. Early iterations of chatbots, such as ELIZA in the 1960s, were rudimentary programs that followed predefined scripts. ELIZA was capable of simulating a conversation based on patterns and keyword recognition, but it lacked true understanding. Over the years, chatbots evolved to incorporate more complex algorithms, natural language processing (NLP), and machine learning models. These advancements have allowed chatbots to interpret and respond to user input in a way that mimics human dialogue more effectively, which has made them increasingly useful in a wide range of industries, from customer service to healthcare and e-commerce. Today's chatbots are often integrated into websites, mobile apps, and messaging platforms, enabling users to engage in interactive conversations to solve problems, obtain information, or complete tasks.

Virtual assistants, on the other hand, represent a more advanced form of chatbot, typically with greater capabilities for performing tasks and managing information. Popular examples like Apple's Siri, Amazon's Alexa, and Google Assistant have become household names, providing users with the ability to interact with their devices using voice commands. Virtual assistants leverage sophisticated AI models, including machine learning and deep learning, to process and understand voice input and respond accordingly. These systems are capable of performing a variety of tasks, such as setting reminders, providing weather forecasts, controlling smart home devices, playing music, and even assisting with online shopping. The advent of virtual assistants has made them indispensable tools in everyday life, especially with the rise of smart speakers and other connected devices. In addition to voice-based communication, many virtual assistants can integrate with other services and applications, allowing users to streamline their daily routines and interact with various platforms seamlessly. The success of virtual assistants is due in large part to their ability to understand context, improve their responses over time, and offer personalized recommendations based on user behaviour and preferences. As AI continues to improve, the functionality of virtual assistants will likely expand, potentially becoming even more integrated into daily life and offering an increasingly sophisticated level of support.

Emotional AI, also known as affective computing or emotion AI, is an area of AI research focused on enabling machines to recognize, interpret, and simulate human emotions. This type of AI adds a layer of emotional intelligence to virtual assistants and chatbots, allowing them to go beyond just understanding language to also gauge the emotional state of the user. Emotional AI relies on advanced algorithms, including facial recognition, voice sentiment analysis, and physiological data interpretation, to assess emotions like happiness, sadness, anger, or frustration. The integration of emotional intelligence into AI systems enhances their ability to respond in a more empathetic and contextually appropriate manner. For instance, if a chatbot detects that a user is frustrated or upset, it might offer a more sympathetic or calming response, which could improve the user's overall experience. Similarly, virtual assistants that are emotionally aware could adjust their tone or phrasing based on the emotional context of the conversation. This form of emotional awareness is crucial in settings where human-like interaction is important, such as in mental health applications, customer service, or eldercare. Emotional AI is also being integrated into technologies like robotics and virtual reality, where creating a sense of connection between humans and machines is essential for creating immersive and engaging experiences.

One of the primary benefits of emotional AI is its potential to improve user experience by adding a layer of empathy to interactions with machines. This can make conversations feel more natural and meaningful, especially in areas like customer support, where human-like responses are often needed to resolve issues effectively. For example, a chatbot equipped with emotional AI could not only provide information but also adjust its responses based on the tone of the user's queries, helping to defuse tense situations. In customer service, this emotional intelligence can lead to more positive outcomes, as customers feel heard and understood, leading to higher satisfaction and loyalty. In healthcare, emotionally aware virtual assistants could offer support for individuals dealing with mental health issues by recognizing when a user is distressed and offering appropriate coping mechanisms or resources. However, there are also challenges and ethical concerns surrounding the development of emotional AI. One issue is the potential for misuse or manipulation. Emotional AI systems can be designed to influence emotions or guide behaviour, which raises questions about privacy, consent, and transparency. For instance, if an emotional AI system detects a user's vulnerability, it could potentially exploit this to market products or services. Ensuring that these technologies are used responsibly and ethically is a critical concern as they become more prevalent.

The intersection of chatbots, virtual assistants, and emotional AI opens up new possibilities for creating more human-like interactions with machines. While chatbots and virtual assistants are already prevalent in many aspects of modern life, the incorporation of emotional AI has the potential to further transform these systems, making them not only more intelligent but also more compassionate. For example, emotionally aware virtual assistants could provide tailored recommendations not only based on past behaviour but also considering the emotional state of the user at the time of the request. This could be particularly useful in applications such as mental health apps, where understanding a person's mood or emotional state is crucial for providing appropriate support or guidance. Similarly, in customer service, a chatbot equipped with emotional AI could handle sensitive situations with greater sensitivity, reducing frustration and improving customer satisfaction. By blending cognitive abilities with emotional intelligence, these technologies could bridge the gap between human and machine interaction, making it easier for users to engage with AI systems in a way that feels more intuitive and natural.

Despite their potential, there are still challenges to overcome in perfecting these technologies. For instance, while emotional AI can recognize and respond to emotions, it is still far from achieving the nuance and complexity of human emotional understanding. Emotions are multifaceted and deeply personal, shaped by individual experiences and context, which makes it difficult for machines to fully comprehend them in the way humans do. Furthermore, training AI systems to accurately interpret emotions in a wide range of contexts—across different cultures, languages, and environments—presents significant challenges. There are also concerns around the accuracy of emotional AI's emotional assessments. For instance, AI systems that rely on facial recognition or voice analysis may not always correctly interpret a person's emotional state, particularly in cases where cultural differences or individual idiosyncrasies influence emotional expression. As a result, emotional AI systems may occasionally misinterpret a user's mood or respond inappropriately, which could lead to frustration or confusion.

Looking ahead, the future of chatbots, virtual assistants, and emotional AI is full of exciting possibilities. As machine learning algorithms improve and more data becomes available, these technologies will continue to evolve and become more effective at understanding and engaging with users. In particular, emotional AI holds the promise of creating more empathetic and personalized user experiences, which could have a profound impact on fields such as healthcare, customer service, and education. However, there will need to be ongoing research and development to address the ethical, technical, and societal challenges posed by these technologies. Ensuring that emotional AI is used responsibly, respects privacy, and serves the best interests of users will be key to unlocking its full potential. In the coming years, we can expect chatbots, virtual assistants, and emotional AI to become more integrated into our daily lives, transforming the way we interact with technology and each other.

This overview touches on key aspects of chatbots, virtual assistants, and emotional AI, covering their development, use cases, benefits, challenges, and the future outlook for these technologies.

Risks of AI replacing human relationships

The growing integration of artificial intelligence (AI) into various aspects of human life raises significant concerns, particularly about the potential risks of AI replacing human relationships. While AI technologies have undeniably enhanced convenience, efficiency, and access to information, there is a pressing need to explore the social and psychological implications of allowing machines to play roles traditionally occupied by human beings. One of the fundamental risks of AI replacing human relationships lies in the erosion of emotional depth and empathy that humans inherently share with one another. Human relationships, whether familial, romantic, or social, are built upon the ability to understand, empathize with, and respond to the emotions, needs, and aspirations of others. These relationships are deeply rooted in complex biological, emotional, and cognitive processes that cannot be replicated by AI. AI, by contrast, is designed to respond to patterns and algorithms, rather than the nuanced subtleties of human feelings. Even though AI can simulate empathy to some extent, such as by offering comforting words or mimicking gestures, it lacks the true capacity for emotional connection. This deficiency can create a sense of loneliness or emotional detachment among individuals who rely too heavily on AI systems for companionship and support, ultimately eroding the quality of human relationships.

Moreover, AI's potential to replace human interactions extends beyond companionship and into critical aspects of social engagement, such as decision-making, caregiving, and education. In environments like schools and workplaces, where human connection fosters collaboration, trust, and growth, the use of AI in place of human interaction can lead to a reduction in these essential dynamics. For example, in education, AI-driven systems can provide personalized learning experiences, but they cannot replace the mentorship and emotional guidance that a teacher offers. Teachers not only impart knowledge but also nurture a student's emotional development, encourage creativity, and offer personalized feedback based on the student's unique personality and circumstances. In workplaces, human collaboration fosters innovation and problem-solving, as employees draw from their diverse perspectives and emotional intelligence. AI can support these efforts, but it cannot replace the organic and dynamic relationships that drive teamwork and collective success. By leaning too heavily on AI in these settings, there is a risk of creating environments where individuals are isolated or alienated from their peers, ultimately hindering their personal and professional growth.

In addition to the erosion of emotional and social bonds, there are broader societal risks that stem from AI replacing human relationships. One such concern is the exacerbation of inequality. The widespread use of AI systems for companionship or caregiving could disproportionately impact vulnerable groups, such as the elderly, those with disabilities, and individuals experiencing social isolation. While AI might offer a convenient and accessible solution for providing care or alleviating loneliness, it does so at the expense of real human connection.

The elderly, for instance, may rely on AI companions to combat feelings of loneliness or assist with daily tasks, but this can lead to further isolation as they disengage from interactions with family, friends, and caregivers. As a result, these individuals may miss out on the emotional benefits of human relationships, which are crucial for maintaining mental and physical well-being. Furthermore, the reliance on AI as a surrogate for human care could lead to a reduction in the demand for human caregivers, potentially displacing jobs in industries that rely on human labour, such as healthcare and elder care. This technological displacement could exacerbate economic inequality, as those who depend on these jobs for income may struggle to find new employment opportunities in an AI-driven economy.

Another significant risk of AI replacing human relationships is the potential for increased surveillance and the loss of privacy. Many AI systems rely on vast amounts of personal data to function effectively, whether for personalized recommendations, targeted advertising, or even emotional support. In scenarios where AI is used to replace human relationships, individuals may feel compelled to disclose more personal information to the system in exchange for companionship or care. Over time, this data can be exploited for commercial purposes, or worse, used by malicious actors for nefarious purposes, such as identity theft or manipulation. This growing reliance on AI for personal and emotional needs raises critical questions about the ethical implications of data collection and the boundaries between privacy and accessibility. The erosion of privacy in AI-driven relationships may lead to a sense of vulnerability, as individuals become increasingly aware that their personal information is constantly being monitored, analysed, and stored. In the worst-case scenario, AI systems could become tools for mass surveillance, subtly influencing the decisions, beliefs, and behaviours of individuals based on the data they generate. This poses a significant threat to individual autonomy and freedoms, particularly in societies where the use of AI is not adequately regulated.

The psychological impact of AI replacing human relationships also warrants serious consideration. As AI becomes more integrated into daily life, people may begin to form emotional attachments to machines, perceiving them as genuine sources of companionship, affection, and support. These attachments, however, are often one-sided, with AI systems offering conditional responses based on predefined algorithms. While the interaction may initially feel rewarding, the lack of reciprocity and genuine emotional engagement could ultimately lead to a sense of disillusionment or despair. Individuals who rely on AI for emotional fulfilment may struggle to navigate the complexities of real-life relationships, as they become accustomed to the predictability and control offered by AI systems. Over time, this could result in a diminished capacity for empathy, vulnerability, and authentic human connection. As people invest more time and energy into AI-driven relationships, they may find it increasingly difficult to relate to others in meaningful ways, leading to social withdrawal and an overall decline in mental health.

Furthermore, the risk of AI replacing human relationships is compounded by the growing reliance on AI in the context of work and social interactions. With the rise of virtual assistants, automated customer service, and AI-driven social media algorithms, many people now engage with machines in ways that were once reserved for human contact. While AI may improve efficiency in certain tasks, it also introduces the possibility of reducing the depth and authenticity of human interactions. In the workplace, for instance, employees may find themselves communicating more frequently with AI systems than with their colleagues, diminishing opportunities for collaboration, mentorship, and emotional support. In social media, AI algorithms determine the content individuals see, shaping their perceptions of reality and potentially reinforcing biases or creating echo chambers. The result is a growing fragmentation of human experiences, where individuals are increasingly isolated in their own digital bubbles, interacting with algorithms rather than real people. This shift could further erode the social fabric, weakening the collective sense of community and shared responsibility that binds society together.

Lastly, the potential for AI to replace human relationships raises significant questions about the future of human identity. If individuals begin to rely more on AI for companionship and social interaction, there may be profound consequences for the way people define themselves in relation to others. Relationships are central to human identity, offering opportunities for self-expression, personal growth, and the development of shared meaning. As AI takes on an increasingly central role in social life, the question arises: will individuals begin to value their relationships with machines more than their relationships with other humans? This shift could lead to an existential crisis, where the boundaries between human and machine become blurred, and individuals struggle to reconcile their humanity with the artificial nature of their social interactions. In this context, the erosion of human relationships could have far-reaching consequences, not only for individuals but for society as a whole, as it risks undermining the very essence of what it means to be human.

In conclusion, while AI has the potential to revolutionize many aspects of life, its growing role in replacing human relationships presents significant risks. These include the erosion of emotional depth, the exacerbation of social inequality, the loss of privacy, the psychological impact of one-sided relationships, and the potential for societal fragmentation. As AI continues to evolve, it is crucial to carefully consider the ethical, social, and psychological implications of allowing machines to replace human connections. Rather than viewing AI as a substitute for human relationships, it should be seen as a tool to enhance and complement the depth of human connection, ensuring that it supports rather than diminishes the bonds that make us truly human.

Chapter 8: AI and Education

In the ever-evolving landscape of modern education, artificial intelligence (AI) is playing an increasingly transformative role, influencing teaching methods, learning processes, and the educational experience itself. As we move into the digital age, AI offers promising advancements that can revolutionize the way educational systems operate and how students engage with knowledge. Chapter 8 delves into the multifaceted impact of AI on education, exploring its applications, potential benefits, challenges, and implications for the future of learning. This chapter highlights not only the technological innovations in educational tools and platforms but also the ethical considerations and societal impacts that come with integrating AI into educational settings.

AI has the potential to enhance education in numerous ways, from personalized learning experiences to the automation of administrative tasks. One of the most significant advantages of AI in education is its ability to provide personalized learning pathways for students. Traditional educational models often adopt a one-size-fits-all approach, which may not cater to the individual learning needs of each student. AI, however, can tailor educational content and assessments to the learner's pace, strengths, weaknesses, and preferences. With the use of AI-powered platforms and algorithms, students can receive real-time feedback, customized assignments, and instructional content that align with their specific learning needs. This personalized approach can increase student engagement and improve learning outcomes by ensuring that no student is left behind, regardless of their starting point or learning style.

Moreover, AI-driven tools can help identify patterns in student performance, allowing educators to intervene more effectively. For instance, AI can track a student's progress over time, analysing data points such as test scores, assignment completion rates, and engagement levels. This data can then be used to predict potential areas of difficulty, enabling teachers to provide timely support or adjust their teaching methods. Furthermore, AI can help with early detection of learning disabilities or other challenges, providing educators with insights that might not be immediately apparent through traditional observation. By using AI in this way, educators can be more proactive in addressing students' needs and ensuring that they receive the support necessary for success.

Another key aspect of AI's role in education is its ability to automate administrative tasks, allowing educators to focus more on teaching and student interaction. Teachers often spend a significant portion of their time on administrative duties, such as grading assignments, managing schedules, and tracking attendance. AI can streamline these processes by automating tasks like grading, scheduling, and even generating reports. For example, AI-powered systems can grade assignments, quizzes, and even essays by analysing patterns and using natural language processing techniques to assess student responses. This not only saves teachers valuable time but also ensures that grading is consistent, objective, and free from human bias. By reducing the administrative burden, AI allows teachers to dedicate more time to direct interaction with students, fostering a more dynamic and engaging learning environment.

Despite the many potential benefits of AI in education, there are several challenges and concerns that need to be addressed. One major concern is the digital divide, which refers to the gap between those who have access to advanced technology and those who do not. While AI-powered tools and platforms can enhance learning, they require reliable internet access and modern computing devices. Students from low-income families or rural areas may not have access to the necessary technology, exacerbating existing inequalities in education. To mitigate this issue, governments and educational institutions must ensure that all students have equitable access to the tools and resources needed to benefit from AI-driven education. This includes providing affordable internet access, offering devices for students in need, and investing in infrastructure to support the widespread adoption of AI in schools.

Another challenge is the potential for AI to perpetuate or even exacerbate existing biases in education. AI systems rely on data to make decisions, and if the data used to train these systems contains biases—whether based on race, gender, socioeconomic status, or other factors—the AI may inadvertently reinforce these biases in its recommendations or assessments. For instance, an AI system used for admissions or hiring purposes may be biased toward certain demographic groups if it is trained on historical data that reflects past prejudices. To avoid this, it is essential for developers and educators to be mindful of the data used to train AI systems and to regularly audit these systems for bias. Furthermore, AI must be designed with fairness and inclusivity in mind, ensuring that all students have equal opportunities to succeed.

Ethical concerns surrounding AI in education also include issues related to privacy and data security. AI systems often collect and analyse large amounts of personal data about students, including their academic performance, behaviours, and interactions with digital learning platforms. While this data can be used to improve learning experiences, it also raises concerns about how that data is stored, shared, and protected. Educational institutions and AI developers must prioritize the privacy and security of student data, ensuring that it is used responsibly and in compliance with relevant laws and regulations. Additionally, transparency is key—students and parents should be informed about what data is being collected and how it will be used. By addressing these privacy concerns, AI can be deployed in a way that respects students' rights and safeguards their personal information.

Looking to the future, AI's impact on education is expected to expand, with the potential to further transform how students learn and how educators teach. One of the most exciting possibilities is the integration of AI with emerging technologies such as virtual reality (VR) and augmented reality (AR). These technologies have the potential to create immersive learning environments where students can engage with content in more interactive and hands-on ways. For example, AI-powered VR simulations could allow students to explore historical events, conduct scientific experiments, or experience complex mathematical concepts in a virtual environment. These immersive experiences could make learning more engaging, memorable, and effective, especially for students who struggle with traditional learning methods.

Moreover, AI is likely to play an increasingly important role in lifelong learning and adult education. As the job market continues to evolve, workers will need to acquire new skills throughout their careers. AI-powered platforms can help facilitate this process by offering personalized training programs, providing real-time feedback, and offering flexible learning schedules. Whether for career development, upskilling, or personal enrichment, AI has the potential to democratize access to education for people of all ages and backgrounds.

In conclusion, the integration of AI into education presents a wealth of opportunities and challenges. On the one hand, AI can enhance personalized learning, improve administrative efficiency, and provide valuable insights into student progress. On the other hand, it raises concerns about inequality, bias, privacy, and the ethical use of data. As educational institutions, policymakers, and technology developers continue to explore the potential of AI, it is essential to address these challenges thoughtfully and inclusively. With careful implementation, AI has the potential to reshape the future of education, making it more personalized, accessible, and effective for all learners, regardless of their background or circumstances. The future of education, with AI at its core, holds great promise, but it is essential that we approach it with caution, ensuring that the benefits are widely shared and that no student is left behind.

Personalized learning and AI tutors

Personalized learning has become an increasingly significant concept in education, aiming to tailor educational experiences to meet the unique needs, interests, and abilities of each student. The traditional, one-size-fits-all approach to education often falls short in addressing the diverse learning styles, paces, and challenges that students encounter. Personalized learning offers a solution by utilizing data-driven insights and adaptive technologies to create customized learning pathways that empower students to take ownership of their educational journey. One of the most exciting innovations that have emerged in the realm of personalized learning is the use of Artificial Intelligence (AI) tutors.

These AI-driven systems promise to transform how students interact with educational content, providing tailored support and guidance that evolves with the learner's progress. By leveraging sophisticated algorithms and vast amounts of data, AI tutors are able to provide dynamic, real-time feedback and adapt to the needs of individual students. This integration of AI in education is not merely a passing trend; it has the potential to significantly improve learning outcomes, increase engagement, and enhance accessibility.

AI tutors are powered by machine learning (ML) algorithms, which enable them to analyse vast amounts of data about student behaviour, learning progress, and performance. These systems collect information from a variety of sources, including assessments, quizzes, assignments, and interactions with educational content, to build a comprehensive understanding of the student's learning needs. By continuously monitoring this data, AI tutors can adjust the content, difficulty level, and pace of lessons to suit the learner's specific needs. For example, if a student struggles with a particular concept or skill, the AI tutor can offer additional explanations, practice exercises, and targeted interventions to help the student master the material. This level of personalization is difficult, if not impossible, to achieve in a traditional classroom setting, where teachers must manage the needs of many students simultaneously.

One of the most compelling aspects of AI tutors is their ability to provide instant, individualized feedback. In traditional educational settings, students often have to wait for teachers to grade assignments or provide feedback on their work, which can delay the learning process. With AI tutors, students can receive immediate responses to their questions, helping them identify mistakes and correct misconceptions on the spot. This instant feedback loop allows students to engage in a continuous learning process, making adjustments and improvements in real-time. Furthermore, the personalized feedback provided by AI tutors can be tailored to the specific learning style of each student. For instance, visual learners may benefit from diagrams and videos, while auditory learners might prefer spoken explanations or interactive discussions. AI tutors can adjust their approach

189

based on these preferences, ensuring that the student receives the most effective form of feedback.

The ability of AI tutors to adapt to the individual needs of students also extends to their capacity for differentiated instruction. In a traditional classroom, students often receive the same content at the same pace, regardless of their varying levels of understanding or ability. This can lead to frustration for students who need more time to grasp certain concepts and boredom for those who grasp the material quickly and are not sufficiently challenged. AI tutors address this issue by providing differentiated learning experiences that cater to students at different levels. For instance, an AI tutor might offer more challenging exercises to a student who excels in a particular subject while providing additional support to a student who is struggling. This approach ensures that all students are appropriately challenged and supported, helping them progress at their own pace.

Moreover, AI tutors can also enhance the learning experience by providing students with a more engaging and interactive environment.

Traditional textbooks and worksheets often fail to capture students' attention or keep them motivated throughout the learning process. In contrast, AI-powered systems can incorporate gamification, interactive simulations, and multimedia content to create a more dynamic and engaging learning experience. These interactive features not only make learning more enjoyable but also foster deeper understanding and retention of knowledge. For example, an AI tutor might use virtual simulations to help students visualize complex scientific concepts or employ role-playing games to teach history or language skills. By immersing students in these interactive learning experiences, AI tutors can help them develop a more robust understanding of the subject matter.

While AI tutors offer numerous advantages, they also present challenges and limitations that must be addressed to fully realize their potential. One of the main concerns is the issue of equity and access. Not all students have equal access to the technology required to use AI tutors, such as high-speed internet, computers, or mobile devices. This digital divide could exacerbate existing inequalities in education, with students from lower-income families or rural areas being left behind. To address this issue, policymakers and educational institutions must work to ensure that all students have access to the technology and resources needed for personalized learning. This may involve investing in infrastructure, providing subsidized devices, or exploring alternative methods of delivering AI-based education, such as through offline applications or mobile-friendly platforms.

Another concern is the potential for AI tutors to replace human teachers. While AI has the potential to revolutionize education, it is unlikely to completely replace the role of teachers. Instead, AI tutors should be viewed as complementary tools that can assist educators in meeting the diverse needs of their students. Teachers bring essential qualities to the classroom, such as emotional intelligence, creativity, and the ability to build relationships with students. AI tutors, on the other hand, excel at providing personalized, data-driven feedback and can help alleviate the burden on teachers by handling routine tasks such as grading and assessment. By working together, teachers and AI tutors can create a more effective and efficient learning environment.

Another challenge with AI tutors lies in ensuring that the data they collect is used ethically and securely. AI systems rely heavily on data to function effectively, and this data often includes sensitive information about students' learning behaviours, academic performance, and even personal preferences. It is crucial that this data is handled with care to protect students' privacy and ensure that it is used responsibly. Educational institutions and technology providers must establish clear guidelines and safeguards to protect student data, and they must be transparent about how data is collected, stored, and used. Moreover, AI tutors should be designed to be transparent and explainable, so that students, teachers, and parents can understand how the system is making decisions and recommendations.

Despite these challenges, the potential of AI tutors to revolutionize personalized learning is immense. As technology continues to advance, AI-powered education systems are likely to become more sophisticated and accessible, offering even greater opportunities for individualized learning. For instance, future AI tutors may incorporate natural language processing and emotion recognition to better understand and respond to students' needs. These systems could detect when a student is frustrated or disengaged and provide appropriate interventions to re-engage them in the learning process. Additionally, AI tutors could be integrated with other technologies, such as virtual and augmented reality, to create immersive learning experiences that further enhance student engagement and understanding.

In conclusion, personalized learning and AI tutors represent a powerful combination that has the potential to transform education. By tailoring learning experiences to the individual needs, interests, and abilities of students, AI tutors can provide a more engaging, effective, and efficient learning environment. While challenges such as equity, access, and data privacy must be addressed, the benefits of AI-powered personalized learning are clear. With continued investment in technology, infrastructure, and ethical practices, AI tutors can help create a future of education that is more inclusive, personalized, and responsive to the needs of all learners. The integration of AI in education is not just a trend but a fundamental shift that promises to reshape the way we teach and learn for generations to come.

How AI is changing traditional education models

The landscape of education is undergoing a significant transformation due to the integration of Artificial Intelligence (AI) technologies. Historically, education systems worldwide have adhered to traditional methods of teaching, with rigid structures of teacher-centered instruction, standardized testing, and uniform curriculums. However, AI is challenging these conventional models, opening the door to more personalized, efficient, and data-driven approaches. At the heart of this change is the ability of AI to tailor learning experiences to individual student needs, paving the way for a more customized approach to education. Traditionally, classrooms have struggled with one-size-fits-all teaching, where students of varying learning paces and styles are often taught using the same methods and materials. AI-powered tools, however, allow educators to better understand their students' strengths, weaknesses, preferences, and learning styles. With the help of AI, teachers can now leverage algorithms to provide personalized lesson plans, adaptive learning pathways, and real-time feedback, ensuring that every student receives the support they need to succeed.

One of the most significant changes AI brings to traditional education models is the personalization of learning. In conventional systems, students are often grouped by age and grade level, regardless of their individual learning abilities. This can lead to disengagement for students who either advance too quickly or struggle to keep up with the pace of their peers. With AI, however, educational tools and platforms can analyse a student's past performance, learning speed, and areas of interest to create a more individualized learning experience. For instance, adaptive learning systems powered by AI, such as DreamBox or Knewton, adjust the difficulty of tasks based on a student's responses, offering challenges that are appropriate to their current level of understanding. As a result, students are neither bored by content that is too easy nor frustrated by material that is too complex. This personalized approach fosters a more engaging and motivating learning environment, which is particularly beneficial for students with unique educational needs, including those with learning disabilities, those who are gifted, or those who speak English as a second language.

In addition to personalized learning, AI is also revolutionizing the way educational content is delivered. Traditional classroom instruction has often been dependent on textbooks, lectures, and face-to-face interactions between teachers and students. While these methods can be effective, they do not fully utilize the potential of technology to enhance the learning process. AI-powered platforms, such as interactive tutors, virtual assistants, and language models, are enabling more dynamic and interactive learning experiences. For example, AI-driven chatbots like Squirrel AI provide students with a conversational interface, where they can ask questions and receive instant, contextually relevant answers. These systems are often available 24/7, meaning students can learn at their own pace, outside of traditional school hours. Additionally, AI has facilitated the development of immersive learning environments, such as virtual reality (VR) and augmented reality (AR), which allow students to interact with complex subjects in ways that were previously unimaginable. In a history class, for example, students could virtually tour ancient civilizations, or in a science class, they could conduct experiments in a virtual lab. These technologies expand the boundaries of traditional education, offering engaging, hands-on experiences that were once limited to expensive field trips or specialized equipment.

Another key benefit of AI in education is the enhancement of teacher productivity. Teachers, despite their dedication, often face heavy workloads that can limit the amount of time they can devote to each student. Grading papers, preparing lesson plans, and managing classroom dynamics take up a significant portion of their time, leaving less opportunity for personalized instruction. AI can alleviate some of these burdens by automating administrative tasks such as grading, scheduling, and resource allocation. AI-powered systems can instantly grade multiple-choice tests or essays, providing teachers with more time to focus on areas where human intervention is needed. For example, automated grading tools like Gradescope use machine learning to grade written responses, giving instructors more time to engage with students on a deeper level. Furthermore, AI can assist in monitoring classroom behaviour, identifying students who might need additional support, and even predicting which students may be at risk of falling behind academically. Teachers can use these insights to intervene early, helping students get back on track before their struggles become more pronounced.

The use of AI is also transforming the way educational institutions approach assessment and evaluation. Traditional education models often rely on standardized testing as a primary means of assessing student achievement. However, standardized tests have been criticized for their inability to account for individual differences in learning and intelligence, as well as their narrow focus on memorization and test-taking skills. AI presents an alternative to this model by providing continuous and more accurate forms of assessment. AI tools can track students' progress over time, offering real-time feedback and detailed analytics on their performance across a variety of activities, from quizzes and essays to discussions and project work. Instead of relying solely on one-time assessments, AI enables educators to gain a more holistic understanding of each student's abilities and progress. These insights allow for more dynamic and formative assessments that can guide both students and teachers in improving the learning experience. Additionally, AI has the potential to address the biases often associated with traditional assessments. By removing human subjectivity from grading, AI ensures that students are evaluated fairly, based solely on their knowledge and performance.

While AI is undoubtedly transforming the educational landscape, it also raises important challenges and concerns. One of the primary concerns is the digital divide, which refers to the disparity in access to technology and internet connectivity among students from different socioeconomic backgrounds. While AI-based educational tools can be incredibly effective, they often require access to high-quality devices and reliable internet connections, which may not be available to all students. In some cases, this can exacerbate existing inequalities in education, as students from underprivileged backgrounds may not be able to fully participate in AI-driven learning opportunities. Addressing this digital divide is essential to ensuring that AI's potential benefits are equitably distributed among all students. Furthermore, there are concerns about data privacy and security, as AI systems often require large amounts of personal data to function effectively. Schools and educational institutions must prioritize data protection measures to ensure that students' information is not misused or compromised. Another challenge is the potential for over-reliance on AI, which could lead to the erosion of human interaction in the classroom. Teachers are not only educators but also mentors and role models, and AI cannot replace the essential human connection that is fundamental to the educational experience. Striking a balance between utilizing AI tools and preserving the human element of teaching will be critical as AI continues to play a larger role in education.

The future of AI in education is undeniably exciting, with numerous possibilities for enhancing teaching and learning. As AI continues to evolve, it is likely that educational models will become increasingly dynamic, flexible, and responsive to the needs of students. Personalized learning pathways will become more refined, allowing for more accurate predictions of student success and more targeted interventions. Moreover, AI will likely play a key role in the development of lifelong learning, as adults continue to seek new skills and knowledge throughout their careers. Online learning platforms, powered by AI, can help individuals of all ages and backgrounds pursue education in a way that fits their schedule and learning style. In the future, AI may even enable highly advanced simulations and immersive experiences, allowing students to participate in virtual apprenticeships, collaborative projects, and international learning exchanges without leaving their homes. The growing role of AI in education is not just about improving access to knowledge but also about rethinking the very nature of learning itself.

In conclusion, AI is fundamentally changing traditional education models by making learning more personalized, interactive, and data-driven. By enabling personalized learning experiences, automating administrative tasks, and providing more accurate and continuous assessments, AI has the potential to improve outcomes for students, educators, and institutions alike. However, the integration of AI in education also raises significant challenges, such as the digital divide, data privacy concerns, and the need to maintain the human touch in teaching. Moving forward, it will be essential to address these challenges while embracing the opportunities AI offers to create a more inclusive, engaging, and effective education system for the future. As AI continues to evolve, it is likely that its role in education will only grow, fundamentally reshaping how we learn, teach, and think about knowledge in the years to come.

Challenges and limitations of AI in learning

The integration of Artificial Intelligence (AI) into learning environments has opened up a plethora of opportunities to enhance educational processes. AI tools promise personalized learning experiences, efficient data analysis, and dynamic content creation. However, despite the remarkable advancements, several challenges and limitations accompany AI's application in learning systems. These challenges span various domains, including ethical considerations, technical issues, the need for human interaction, and the limitations imposed by AI's current capabilities. In this essay, we will explore some of the key hurdles in implementing AI into education systems, the obstacles teachers and students face, and the implications these limitations have for the future of AI in learning.

Ethical Considerations and Bias in AI Systems

One of the most significant challenges facing AI in learning is the ethical concerns related to its use. AI systems, particularly those that employ machine learning algorithms, are inherently susceptible to biases, often based on the data used to train them. These biases can have a significant impact on the learning experience, especially in contexts like student assessment, recommendation systems, and content creation. For example, if an AI system is trained on data that underrepresents certain demographic groups, the AI may inadvertently Favor or disadvantage students from those groups. This could result in inequitable educational experiences, reinforcing existing disparities in access to quality education. Moreover, the data used to train these systems may also reflect historical and social biases, which are then perpetuated in the AI's decisions and recommendations.

Furthermore, there are concerns related to privacy and data security. AI systems require vast amounts of personal data, such as students' learning habits, behaviour patterns, and performance metrics, to function effectively. This raises concerns about how this sensitive information is stored, who has access to it, and whether it is used appropriately. Mismanagement or misuse of this data could lead to significant violations of privacy and create security risks, especially if the data is hacked or exposed. These issues complicate the widespread adoption of AI in learning environments, as many stakeholders—teachers, students, parents, and regulatory bodies—demand greater transparency, accountability, and security regarding AI systems' operations.

Lack of Human Interaction and Emotional Intelligence

Another limitation of AI in learning is its inability to replicate the complex emotional intelligence that human teachers bring to the classroom. While AI can offer personalized learning paths, provide real-time feedback, and track progress, it lacks the nuanced understanding of human emotions and the ability to respond empathetically. Learning is not purely a cognitive process—it involves social and emotional dimensions that are critical to student engagement, motivation, and overall well-being. A teacher can detect when a student is frustrated, anxious, or disengaged and adjust their approach accordingly, something that AI cannot currently do.

The absence of emotional intelligence in AI means that the human touch, which is essential in fostering a positive learning environment, is missing. Students may feel alienated or unsupported by an AI system that cannot perceive their emotional state or understand the socio-cultural factors that influence their learning. Additionally, students often benefit from the mentorship and guidance of teachers, which provides emotional support that is critical for their personal and academic development. This human connection, built on trust and understanding, is something that AI systems are far from replicating in a meaningful way.

Technological and Infrastructure Limitations

AI's implementation in education is also hindered by technological and infrastructure limitations. For AI systems to function effectively, they require significant computational power, access to large datasets, and high-quality algorithms. These resources may not be readily available in many educational institutions, particularly those in underfunded or rural areas. Schools with limited budgets may struggle to implement AI-based learning tools or invest in the necessary infrastructure, such as high-speed internet, to fully leverage these technologies. This exacerbates the digital divide, creating a gap between students in well-funded institutions and those in under-resourced areas, thus limiting AI's potential to democratize learning.

Moreover, the reliance on data can be problematic. AI systems require large, high-quality datasets to be trained effectively. In education, however, such datasets are often not readily available, especially when it comes to smaller or underrepresented student populations. This lack of data can limit the accuracy and reliability of AI-driven solutions, leading to flawed conclusions or incorrect recommendations. Additionally, some educational environments may not have the digital literacy necessary to operate AI tools effectively, creating a barrier to access and making it difficult for both educators and students to take full advantage of AI technologies.

Limited Adaptability and Over-Reliance on Data

While AI excels in areas such as pattern recognition and data analysis, its adaptability remains a significant limitation. AI systems often operate within predefined parameters and struggle to adapt to new, unforeseen challenges processes. If the data is incomplete, outdated, or biased, the AI system will produce inaccurate or ineffective results. In learning contexts, this can lead to students receiving incorrect feedback, assessments, or learning recommendations. Over-reliance on data-driven solutions could also undermine creative and critical thinking in students, who might become accustomed to receiving answers from AI systems rather than developing their own problem-solving abilities.

Teacher Resistance and Job Displacement Concerns

The introduction of AI in learning environments often faces resistance from educators, who may fear that AI will replace their roles or devalue their expertise. Teachers play an essential role in guiding students through the learning process, offering emotional support, and providing individualized attention that an AI system may not be able to offer. The fear of job or changes in context. For instance, in a classroom setting, a student may present a learning style or issue that the AI system was not trained to address. AI may not be able to adjust its teaching approach as quickly as a human teacher could, especially in complex, non-linear learning scenarios.

Additionally, AI systems are heavily reliant on data, which can be both a strength and a limitation. The quality of an AI's performance is directly tied to the quality of the data it

displacement is particularly prominent in the face of AI's growing presence, as some worry that automation will make certain teaching roles obsolete. While AI can undoubtedly improve efficiency and assist in routine tasks such as grading and administrative work, it is unlikely to replace teachers entirely.

Furthermore, the rapid pace of technological change often requires teachers to continually update their skills to keep up with new AI tools. This places additional pressure on educators who are already burdened with demanding workloads. Many teachers may feel inadequately trained or supported in using AI effectively, which can limit the technology's potential to enhance learning. Without proper training and integration into the curriculum, AI's benefits may be underutilized, leading to suboptimal results.

Dependence on AI and Its Potential Long-Term Effects

Finally, there is the concern about the long-term impact of AI on students and their development. As AI takes on more responsibility in the classroom, there is a risk that students may become overly dependent on AI-driven tools and lose important skills. For instance, over-reliance on AI for problem-solving or learning assistance may hinder the development of critical thinking and creativity. Students may begin to view AI as the ultimate authority, thus stunting their ability to engage in independent thought and problem-solving.

In the long term, this reliance on AI could foster a generation of learners who are less self-reliant, less adaptable, and less equipped to think critically without technological assistance. Additionally, as AI tools become more integrated into everyday life, students may find it difficult to navigate situations that require human judgment, empathy, and intuition—skills that are not easily replicated by machines. It is essential to strike a balance between leveraging AI for efficiency and fostering the development of human cognitive and emotional intelligence.

Conclusion

While AI offers great potential to transform learning, its limitations and challenges cannot be overlooked. Issues of bias, ethical concerns, lack of emotional intelligence, technological barriers, resistance from educators, and the potential for long-term dependency on AI all pose significant obstacles to its widespread and effective use in education. To address these challenges, it is crucial for policymakers, educators, and technology developers to collaborate in creating AI tools that are transparent, ethical, and capable of complementing, not replacing, the human elements of education. As AI continues to evolve, it will be important to carefully consider its limitations and ensure that it enhances, rather than detracts from, the learning experience.

Chapter 9: AI in Warfare and National Security

The integration of artificial intelligence (AI) into warfare and national security is a transformative shift that is reshaping the strategic and operational dimensions of modern conflict. As technological advancements in AI continue to progress, military leaders and policymakers are increasingly recognizing the profound implications of these innovations in both enhancing defence capabilities and posing new challenges to security dynamics. The chapter delves into the multifaceted role AI is playing in warfare and national security, examining its applications, ethical concerns, operational implications, and the future trajectory of AI in military contexts.

At its core, AI in warfare offers the promise of enhancing efficiency, effectiveness, and precision in a range of military operations. Through the development of autonomous systems, such as drones and unmanned ground vehicles (UGVs), AI has the potential to carry out surveillance, reconnaissance, and even combat missions with minimal human intervention. This shift is not limited to the battlefield but extends into cyber warfare, intelligence gathering, and decision-making processes within command and control systems. Machine learning algorithms can process vast amounts of data far more efficiently than human analysts, providing military leaders with more accurate, real-time intelligence to make informed decisions. AI-driven platforms, including automated drones and robotic soldiers, are capable of executing military strategies with unprecedented speed, thereby altering the calculus of warfare.

However, the incorporation of AI in warfare is not without its ethical dilemmas. The prospect of autonomous weapons systems raises significant concerns about accountability and the potential for unintended consequences. One of the central issues debated in the chapter is the moral implications of delegating life-and-death decisions to machines. While AI systems can be programmed to adhere to strict protocols, their ability to exercise judgment, especially in complex, rapidly changing combat environments, remains a subject of considerable debate. The idea of "killer robots," autonomous weapons that can select and engage targets without human oversight, has sparked global discussions about the need for regulatory frameworks that can prevent such technologies from being misused or inadvertently escalating conflicts.

Beyond ethical concerns, the chapter also examines the strategic implications of AI in warfare. One of the key elements discussed is the impact AI has on the nature of conflict itself. In traditional warfare, the outcome often depends on factors such as manpower, resources, and strategy. With the advent of AI, however, warfare is becoming increasingly asymmetrical. Nations with advanced AI capabilities can gain a significant edge over adversaries who are slower to adopt these technologies. This creates a new type of arms race, not just in terms of physical weapons but in the realm of data and algorithmic power. Countries with superior AI capabilities may be able to conduct more effective cyberattacks, engage in sophisticated psychological operations, or achieve faster and more accurate military responses, thus shifting the balance of power in global security.

Moreover, AI's role in national security extends well beyond the battlefield and into the domain of cybersecurity. As nations become more reliant on digital infrastructure for everything from economic transactions to communication networks, the threat of cyberattacks becomes increasingly significant.

AI offers new ways to defend against cyber threats, enabling rapid detection of anomalies and potential intrusions. Machine learning algorithms can identify emerging attack patterns, allowing for quicker responses to mitigate damage. However, the chapter also highlights the vulnerabilities that AI itself introduces into cybersecurity. While AI can enhance the effectiveness of defensive measures, it can also be weaponized by adversaries to carry out cyberattacks that are difficult to predict and counter. The use of AI in offensive cyber operations could potentially disrupt critical infrastructure, compromise national security, and lead to widespread societal consequences.

AI also plays a crucial role in intelligence gathering and analysis, a function that has become even more critical in the context of modern security challenges. As the volume of data being generated globally continues to increase, AI's ability to process and analyse this data at scale is becoming indispensable for national security agencies. Through natural language processing (NLP) and image recognition, AI systems can sift through vast amounts of intelligence data to identify

218

patterns and detect potential threats. This capability significantly enhances the speed and accuracy of intelligence assessments, enabling intelligence agencies to detect emerging threats before they materialize. However, the sheer volume of data and the potential for AI systems to be overwhelmed by irrelevant or misleading information raises concerns about the reliability and accountability of AI-driven intelligence operations.

Another critical aspect of AI in national security is the potential for its use in psychological warfare. AI-powered systems can be employed to manipulate public opinion, sow discord, or influence political outcomes. Through sophisticated data mining and machine learning algorithms, adversaries can target specific groups with tailored disinformation campaigns designed to create division and confusion. This form of warfare is particularly challenging to counter because it operates in the realm of perception rather than traditional military force. The ability of AI to disseminate fake news, manipulate social media platforms, and amplify extremist ideologies is a growing concern for governments worldwide. The chapter explores the challenges of developing regulatory measures to address the threat posed by AI-driven misinformation while balancing the need for free expression and information flow.

In addition to the immediate concerns of AI in warfare and national security, the chapter also looks at the long-term consequences of these technologies. As AI continues to evolve, the potential for new forms of conflict and instability emerges. The possibility of AI-driven warfare raises the Specter of an arms race in autonomous weapons and cyber capabilities, leading to a scenario where nations may find themselves caught in a cycle of technological escalation. This creates new risks of conflict, where even a small miscalculation or technological failure could lead to unintended military engagements. Furthermore, the proliferation of AI technologies means that non-state actors, including terrorist organizations and rogue states, may gain access to these tools, complicating efforts to maintain global security.

To address these challenges, the chapter calls for a balanced approach to the regulation and oversight of AI in military and national security contexts. While AI presents numerous opportunities for enhancing defence capabilities, there must be safeguards in place to prevent misuse and ensure accountability. International agreements and frameworks, similar to those established for arms control, are needed to establish clear boundaries for the use of AI in warfare. Such agreements should address issues like autonomous weapons, AI-driven cyberattacks, and the ethical use of AI in intelligence operations. Moreover, efforts to ensure transparency and maintain human oversight in critical decision-making processes will be essential in mitigating the risks associated with AI in warfare and national security.

The chapter concludes by emphasizing the need for a multidisciplinary approach to AI in warfare and national security. Policymakers, military leaders, ethicists, and technologists must work together to develop strategies that maximize the benefits of AI while minimizing its risks. This collaboration will be essential in ensuring that AI serves as a tool for peace and security rather than a catalyst for instability. As the role of AI in warfare and national security continues to evolve, it is imperative that nations remain vigilant, adaptable, and committed to developing responsible and ethical approaches to these powerful technologies.

In summary, AI in warfare and national security represents both an unprecedented opportunity and a significant challenge. The technologies driving these advancements have the potential to revolutionize military strategy, enhance national defence, and improve the ability to safeguard global security. However, they also raise profound ethical, strategic, and operational concerns that must be carefully considered. The ongoing development and deployment of AI in these contexts will require a concerted effort from all stakeholders to ensure that its potential is harnessed for the benefit of peace and stability, rather than for the escalation of conflict and risk.

AI in military strategy and defence systems

Artificial Intelligence (AI) is revolutionizing numerous industries, and one of the most profound areas of its impact is in military strategy and defence systems. The integration of AI into military applications is transforming the way nations approach defence, warfare, and national security. AI technologies, such as machine learning, neural networks, and data analysis, are enabling military forces to enhance their decision-making processes, improve operational efficiency, and develop autonomous systems that can operate in complex environments. The use of AI in defence systems is not limited to improving efficiency in existing technologies but also extends to the development of entirely new systems and strategies that were once unimaginable.

One of the key advantages of AI in military strategy is its ability to process and analyse vast amounts of data far more efficiently than human operators. Modern warfare generates enormous quantities of data from a variety of sources, including satellite imagery, intelligence reports, communications, and sensor networks. Traditional methods of analysing this data, which rely on human analysts, can be slow and prone to errors. AI, with its ability to rapidly process and identify patterns in large datasets, can significantly enhance decision-making by providing military leaders with real-time insights and predictions. For example, AI-powered systems can assist in identifying potential threats, assessing the likelihood of success in military operations, and offering tactical recommendations based on real-time data analysis.

In addition to improving decision-making, AI is also playing a critical role in the development of autonomous systems. Unmanned aerial vehicles (UAVs), drones, and autonomous ground vehicles are already being deployed in various military operations, with AI enabling these systems to operate independently or in coordination with human operators. These systems are capable of performing tasks such as surveillance, reconnaissance, and even offensive operations without direct human intervention. The use of AI in these systems reduces the risk to human soldiers and increases the operational effectiveness of military forces. For instance, AI can be used to program drones to carry out surveillance missions, follow predetermined flight paths, and adapt to changing environmental conditions, all without needing human input at every stage.

The potential for AI to enhance the accuracy and precision of weapons systems is another area where its influence is felt. AI can be used to guide precision strikes, ensuring that weapons are deployed effectively and with minimal collateral damage. For example, AI algorithms can be integrated into missile guidance systems, improving targeting accuracy by analysing data from multiple sensors and making real-time adjustments to the missile's flight path. Similarly, AI can help in the development of advanced defence systems, such as anti-missile technologies, by predicting the trajectory of incoming threats and determining the most effective countermeasures. In this way, AI contributes to the creation of more effective and reliable defence systems, which are essential in modern warfare.

Furthermore, AI is helping to reshape military strategy by enabling faster and more adaptive responses to changing battlefield conditions. Traditional military strategies often relied on pre-planned tactics and human decision-making, which could be slow and inflexible in the face of rapidly evolving circumstances. AI, on the other hand, can enable military forces to quickly adapt to new threats and conditions by continuously analysing incoming data and suggesting strategic adjustments in real time. For example, AI can help commanders anticipate enemy movements, predict the outcomes of different tactical approaches, and recommend changes to plans based on the evolving situation on the ground. This ability to rapidly adjust to new information is crucial in modern conflict, where the tempo of operations is faster than ever.

While the integration of AI into military strategy offers numerous advantages, it also raises significant ethical, legal, and strategic challenges. One of the most pressing concerns is the potential for AI to be used in autonomous weapons systems that operate without human oversight. The idea of machines making life-and-death decisions without human intervention raises serious questions about accountability and the potential for unintended consequences. For instance, if an autonomous drone mistakenly targets a civilian area instead of a military installation, who is responsible for the resulting harm? The lack of clear accountability in the use of autonomous systems poses significant ethical challenges that must be addressed before such technologies are widely deployed in warfare.

Moreover, the increasing reliance on AI in military systems raises concerns about the potential for adversaries to develop countermeasures that could exploit vulnerabilities in AI algorithms. The use of AI in defence systems relies on the integrity and security of the underlying software and data. If an enemy can disrupt or manipulate the data that AI systems rely on, it could lead to catastrophic failures in military operations. Additionally, AI systems can be vulnerable to adversarial attacks, where small changes in the input data can lead to incorrect predictions or actions. Ensuring the robustness and security of AI systems in military applications is therefore essential to maintaining their effectiveness in combat situations.

AI's influence in military strategy also extends to the realm of cyber warfare. Cyber threats are increasingly becoming a significant concern for national security, and AI is being used to both defend against and launch cyber-attacks. AI algorithms can be employed to detect and mitigate cyber threats in real-time, identifying patterns of malicious activity that would be difficult for human analysts to detect. On the offensive side, AI can be used to launch sophisticated cyber-attacks that can disrupt an enemy's communications, infrastructure, and military capabilities. As the world becomes more interconnected, the role of AI in cybersecurity and cyber warfare is likely to grow, further complicating the landscape of modern military strategy.

The application of AI in military strategy also has the potential to shift the balance of power in global geopolitics. Nations that are able to effectively harness the power of AI in their defence systems may gain a significant strategic advantage over those that lag behind in adopting these technologies. This potential for AI to reshape military power dynamics is already being recognized by major world powers, who are investing heavily in the development of AI for defence purposes. The race to develop advanced AI technologies has sparked a new arms race, where countries are competing to build more advanced AI-driven military systems to ensure their security and influence on the global stage.

In conclusion, the integration of AI into military strategy and defence systems is bringing about transformative changes in the way modern warfare is conducted. AI's ability to process vast amounts of data, improve decision-making, and enable autonomous systems is enhancing the efficiency and effectiveness of military operations. Additionally, AI is playing a critical role in the development of more precise and accurate weapons systems, as well as providing military forces with the ability to adapt rapidly to changing conditions on the battlefield. However, the increasing reliance on AI in defence systems also raises significant ethical, legal, and strategic challenges that must be addressed. As nations continue to invest in AI for military applications, the potential for AI to reshape global military dynamics and influence the future of warfare is immense. The next frontier of military strategy will undoubtedly be shaped by the continued evolution of AI technologies, which will continue to challenge traditional concepts of warfare, ethics, and international security.

Autonomous weapons and their ethical implications

Autonomous weapons, also known as lethal autonomous weapons systems (LAWS), refer to military systems that can select and engage targets without human intervention. These weapons have garnered significant attention due to their technological capabilities, potential advantages in warfare, and, most notably, their ethical implications. The development of autonomous weapons systems has been driven by advancements in artificial intelligence (AI), machine learning, robotics, and sensor technologies, which enable machines to make decisions independently of human oversight. Proponents of autonomous weapons argue that they could enhance military effectiveness, reduce human casualties in combat, and improve the precision of strikes. However, the ethical concerns surrounding these systems are profound and multifaceted, involving issues of accountability, discrimination, the risk of misuse, and the potential for a destabilizing arms race.

One of the most significant ethical concerns regarding autonomous weapons is the issue of accountability. Traditional warfare involves clear lines of responsibility, with human operators or commanders being held accountable for their decisions, actions, and any resulting consequences. With autonomous weapons, however, this accountability becomes murky. If an autonomous weapon makes a mistake, such as targeting the wrong civilian population or engaging a non-combatant, it is unclear who should be held responsible. Is the responsibility on the creators of the weapon, the military personnel who deployed it, or the machine itself? The lack of accountability for autonomous systems raises concerns about justice and the possibility of war crimes being committed without anyone being held liable. Furthermore, the inability to attribute responsibility for mistakes in warfare challenges the concept of accountability in military operations, undermining the moral and legal frameworks established by international law, including the Geneva Conventions.

Another key ethical issue is the potential for autonomous weapons to violate the principle of distinction, which is a cornerstone of international humanitarian law (IHL). The principle of distinction requires that combatants distinguish between military targets and civilian objects and individuals, and that they only target those directly involved in the conflict. Autonomous weapons, despite being designed to be highly accurate, may still lack the human ability to understand complex, context-dependent situations and to make nuanced judgments about whether a target is legitimate. For instance, distinguishing between combatants and non-combatants in crowded urban environments or identifying the intent behind the actions of a potential target may prove challenging for AI systems. There is also the concern that autonomous weapons could be easily programmed to carry out indiscriminate strikes, disregarding the principle of proportionality, which requires military forces to ensure that collateral damage is not excessive in relation to the anticipated military advantage. If autonomous systems cannot make these complex moral and legal judgments, they could inadvertently escalate conflicts and cause unnecessary harm to civilians.

The risk of an arms race fuelled by autonomous weapons is another ethical dilemma that has raised alarm among scholars, military experts, and human rights advocates. The development of LAWS may trigger a new kind of arms race, where nations feel compelled to develop increasingly advanced autonomous weapons to maintain or gain a military advantage. This scenario could lead to rapid proliferation of autonomous weapons, making them more accessible to not only

233

powerful nations but also rogue states and non-state actors, such as terrorist organizations. The potential for the spread of such technology increases the likelihood of misuse, including the deployment of autonomous weapons in non-traditional or unconventional warfare scenarios. Moreover, the use of autonomous weapons in conflicts could lower the threshold for the use of force, as the risk of human casualties for the attacking party is reduced. This may make it easier for nations to engage in violent actions, leading to greater instability and the risk of escalating conflicts to levels that may have been avoided if human judgment were involved in the decision-making process.

In addition to these concerns, there is the ethical issue of whether machines should be allowed to make life-and-death decisions in the first place. The delegation of such decisions to machines raises profound questions about human dignity, autonomy, and the moral status of artificial intelligence. Some argue that the use of autonomous weapons may reduce the sanctity of life, as the act of killing becomes dehumanized and removed from human decision-making. The reliance on algorithms and decision-making processes based on data and programming could strip away the ethical considerations that guide human action in war. A human being making the decision to use lethal force typically does so with an understanding of the value of life, even in the context of warfare. However, machines operate according to logic and data, without the capacity for empathy, moral reflection, or understanding of the broader consequences of their actions. By removing human agency from life-and-death decisions, the moral responsibility that is traditionally associated with such decisions may be lost, raising concerns about the erosion of humanity in warfare.

The question of whether autonomous weapons can ever be fully trusted to comply with international laws and ethical norms is another aspect of the debate. Proponents of autonomous weapons often argue that the use of AI and machine learning can improve the precision and efficiency of military operations, reducing the likelihood of civilian casualties and unnecessary destruction. However, critics counter that the technology is not yet sufficiently advanced to ensure that autonomous weapons will consistently make ethical decisions in the heat of battle. For example, AI systems are prone to biases based on the data they are trained on, and these biases could manifest in discriminatory targeting or other unintended consequences. Furthermore, there are concerns about the "black box" nature of AI decision-making, where even the creators of the system may not fully understand how or why a particular decision is made by the machine. This lack of transparency raises the possibility of unforeseen outcomes and makes it difficult to hold systems accountable for actions that deviate from established ethical standards.

The potential impact of autonomous weapons on warfare itself is another crucial area of concern. In the future, it is possible that autonomous weapons could change the nature of warfare by making it more remote and impersonal. If large-scale wars are fought by machines, with human involvement limited to overseeing or programming the systems, there may be a greater disconnect between the battlefield and the decision-making process. This disconnection could lead to a detachment from the human costs of war, as military personnel may become less emotionally invested in the outcomes of conflicts. This detachment could result in a dehumanizing effect, where the value of human life is further diminished, and the societal impact of war becomes less apparent. Furthermore, the use of autonomous weapons could blur the lines between war and peace, as states may engage in acts of aggression without the traditional markers of warfare, such as the mobilization of troops and the declaration of war.

Given these ethical challenges, many have called for international regulation or even a ban on the development and use of autonomous weapons. Advocacy groups, such as the Campaign to Stop Killer Robots, argue that autonomous weapons should be prohibited to ensure that humans remain in control of life-and-death decisions. They emphasize the need for human judgment in the use of force, and the risks associated with delegating such decisions to machines. Some countries, including Canada, have called for the establishment of international treaties or agreements to regulate autonomous weapons, drawing parallels with existing conventions that govern chemical, biological, and nuclear weapons. However, there is considerable debate about how to approach the issue. Some argue that a ban is unrealistic, given the technological momentum behind the development of autonomous weapons and the security concerns of states. Instead, they suggest that international agreements should focus on establishing clear guidelines for the use of such weapons, ensuring that they comply with international humanitarian law and ethical standards.

In conclusion, the ethical implications of autonomous weapons are complex and multifaceted, touching upon issues of accountability, responsibility, discrimination, arms proliferation, and the fundamental nature of warfare itself. While autonomous weapons have the potential to revolutionize warfare by improving precision and reducing human casualties, they also pose significant risks, including the possibility of misuse, violations of international law, and the erosion of ethical standards in military decision-making. As the development of these technologies continues, it is crucial that international policymakers, military experts, and ethicists engage in a broad and inclusive discussion about the potential consequences of autonomous weapons and the ethical frameworks that should govern their use. Ensuring that humanity remains in control of the decisions that affect human life is a foundational principle that must be preserved in the age of automation and artificial intelligence.

The role of AI in cyber warfare and intelligence

Artificial Intelligence (AI) has rapidly transformed multiple domains across various industries, and one of the most significant areas where it is making a profound impact is in the realm of cyber warfare and intelligence. The use of AI in these domains is enhancing both offensive and defensive capabilities, enabling faster decision-making, automating complex tasks, and offering new methods of analysis that were previously impossible. Cyber warfare and intelligence operations often involve complex, time-sensitive scenarios where human limitations in processing vast amounts of data or identifying patterns in real time may hinder effective outcomes. AI, with its ability to process large data sets quickly, recognize patterns, and predict future threats, has emerged as a vital tool in helping governments and organizations respond to and mitigate the ever-growing threats in cyberspace.

In cyber warfare, AI can be deployed in both defensive and offensive strategies. On the defensive side, AI is used to enhance cybersecurity systems by identifying and neutralizing potential threats before they can cause damage. AI systems are designed to recognize malicious activities, such as hacking attempts, malware infections, or phishing attacks, by analysing network traffic, user behaviour, and other relevant data. Traditional security systems rely on pre-established rules and patterns to detect suspicious activities, but these systems often struggle to adapt to new, unseen threats. AI, on the other hand, can continuously learn from new data and improve its detection methods, allowing for more proactive defence mechanisms. By utilizing machine learning and deep learning algorithms, AI systems can also predict future vulnerabilities and recommend mitigation strategies, enabling organizations to stay ahead of emerging threats.

On the offensive side, AI has been leveraged to enhance cyber-attacks. Hackers and nation-state actors often use AI-driven tools to automate and scale their attacks, making them faster and more difficult to defend against. AI-powered malware can adapt and modify itself to bypass traditional security measures, learn from its environment, and identify the most effective ways to infiltrate a system. Additionally, AI can be used to create deepfake content, such as videos or audio recordings, that can be used in disinformation campaigns aimed at manipulating public opinion or influencing political outcomes. These tools, combined with the increasing use of the dark web and other covert channels, give cybercriminals and adversarial states more power to disrupt or destroy critical infrastructure, steal sensitive data, or undermine trust in key institutions.

Moreover, AI enhances the capabilities of intelligence agencies, allowing them to process and analyse vast amounts of data to extract valuable insights. Traditional intelligence gathering methods, such as human intelligence (HUMINT) or signals intelligence (SIGINT), are time-consuming and limited by human capacity. AI can process data from a variety of sources, including social media platforms, communications intercepts, and public records, to identify patterns and potential threats. By using natural language processing (NLP) techniques, AI systems can automatically translate and analyse large quantities of text data, such as intercepted communications or open-source intelligence, making it easier for intelligence agencies to detect potential terrorist activities or criminal behaviour. AI's ability to correlate data from multiple sources also aids in identifying trends and connections that may not be immediately obvious to human analysts.

In addition to its role in analysing data, AI can enhance decision-making in intelligence operations by providing real-time recommendations and predictions. AI-driven predictive analytics can be used to anticipate future threats, allowing intelligence agencies to take proactive measures. For example, AI models can analyse patterns in cyber-attacks and predict when and where the next attack might occur, based on historical data. This predictive power allows governments and corporations to fortify their defences before an attack happens. Moreover, AI can assist in tracking and identifying adversarial actors in cyberspace, determining their motives, and forecasting their next moves. By automating routine tasks, AI frees up human intelligence officers to focus on more strategic decisions, enhancing the overall efficiency of intelligence operations.

While AI provides tremendous advantages in the fields of cyber warfare and intelligence, it also raises several concerns and challenges. The increasing reliance on AI systems in cyber defence and intelligence operations presents new vulnerabilities. For instance, adversarial AI could be used to deceive or manipulate AI-powered defence systems, leading to false positives or even the infiltration of secure systems. AI-based systems are not infallible; they are only as effective as the data they are trained on, and there is a risk that biased or incomplete data could lead to incorrect predictions or decisions. The potential for AI to be used in autonomous offensive cyber-attacks also raises ethical and legal concerns. The ability of AI to conduct attacks without human intervention means that cyber warfare could escalate quickly, with little accountability or oversight. Furthermore, the use of AI in cyber warfare may lead to an arms race in cyber capabilities, with states and organizations developing increasingly sophisticated AI tools for both offense and defence.

Ethical concerns regarding privacy and civil liberties are another major issue raised by the application of AI in intelligence operations. The use of AI for mass surveillance, particularly through the analysis of social media or public data, could lead to violations of individuals' privacy rights. Governments may be tempted to use AI to monitor their citizens on a massive scale, raising concerns about state overreach and the erosion of personal freedoms. Additionally, the use of AI in intelligence gathering could potentially be exploited by authoritarian regimes to suppress dissent and control populations. There is also the possibility that AI systems could be used to target specific groups based on biased data or pre-existing stereotypes, further exacerbating social inequalities.

As AI continues to advance, its role in cyber warfare and intelligence will only grow more significant. The integration of AI into the strategic operations of military and intelligence agencies is inevitable, and its impact will continue to reshape how nations approach cyber defence, espionage, and warfare. For example, future AI-driven cyber weapons could include autonomous drones that can identify and neutralize cyber threats in real time or advanced malware that can mimic human behaviour and bypass even the most sophisticated defence mechanisms. These advancements, however, also present challenges in terms of regulating and controlling the use of such technologies. The international community will need to develop new norms, treaties, and regulatory frameworks to ensure that AI is used responsibly and ethically in the context of cyber warfare and intelligence operations.

One potential area of development is the creation of AI systems designed to promote collaboration and information-sharing between countries to combat cyber threats more effectively. Cybersecurity is a global challenge, and AI could play a crucial role in helping nations work together to detect and mitigate cyber-attacks. By pooling data and leveraging AI to identify common threats, countries could create a more unified approach to cybersecurity, reducing the effectiveness of cyber adversaries. This could also help prevent the proliferation of cyber weapons and ensure that AI-driven tools are not used to escalate conflicts. However, such cooperation would require trust and transparency between governments, which could be challenging given the secretive nature of cyber warfare and intelligence operations.

In conclusion, AI is rapidly becoming a central tool in both cyber warfare and intelligence operations, offering powerful capabilities for detecting, preventing, and responding to cyber threats. It enhances the ability to analyse vast quantities of data, automate processes, and predict potential risks, thereby transforming the landscape of cyber defence and intelligence gathering. However, the use of AI in these fields also presents significant risks, including the potential for abuse, ethical concerns, and the escalation of cyber conflicts. As AI technologies continue to evolve, it will be essential for governments, organizations, and international bodies to establish safeguards and regulations that ensure these tools are used responsibly and ethically. Balancing the benefits and risks of AI in cyber warfare and intelligence will require ongoing dialogue, innovation, and cooperation among all stakeholders involved.

Chapter 10: The Role of AI in Climate Change and Sustainability

In recent years, artificial intelligence (AI) has emerged as a transformative technology with the potential to revolutionize multiple sectors, including those dedicated to combating climate change and promoting sustainability. Climate change, a global phenomenon characterized by rising temperatures, extreme weather events, and shifting ecosystems, presents a complex and urgent challenge. Sustainability, meanwhile, involves meeting present needs without compromising the ability of future generations to meet their own. These dual imperatives—addressing climate change and ensuring sustainability—require innovative solutions, and AI has increasingly become a critical tool in the search for such solutions. AI's role in climate change and sustainability can be categorized across several domains, such as climate modelling and forecasting, energy efficiency, agriculture, biodiversity conservation, and waste management. By harnessing the power of machine learning, data analytics, and automation, AI has the potential to contribute significantly to both mitigating the impacts of climate change and advancing sustainable practices.

AI in Climate Modelling and Forecasting

One of the most crucial roles AI plays in the fight against climate change is in the area of climate modelling and forecasting. Climate models are complex systems that simulate the

Earth's climate to predict future conditions based on a range of variables such as atmospheric composition, temperature, and solar radiation. These models are critical for understanding potential climate impacts and informing policy decisions. AI, particularly machine learning (ML), enhances the accuracy and efficiency of climate models by processing vast amounts of data from diverse sources—satellite imagery, weather stations, and historical climate data. Traditional climate models rely heavily on human intuition and computational methods that can be time-consuming and prone to errors. However, AI can analyse large datasets at much faster speeds and identify patterns and correlations that might be too subtle or complex for traditional models to detect.

For example, AI algorithms can be used to predict future climate events such as heatwaves, hurricanes, or droughts with greater precision, which is invaluable for disaster preparedness and mitigation strategies. These advanced predictive capabilities enable better-informed decisions about where and when to allocate resources for disaster relief, ensuring that climate adaptation strategies are more efficient and timely. Additionally, AI can assist in identifying regions most vulnerable to the effects of climate change, helping governments and organizations target their efforts where they are needed most. The integration of AI into climate modelling not only improves the understanding of climate dynamics but also helps policymakers create more resilient and adaptive strategies in the face of changing environmental conditions.

Energy Efficiency and Renewable Energy Integration

Another area where AI plays a significant role is in improving energy efficiency and integrating renewable energy sources into power grids. The transition to renewable energy is central to efforts to combat climate change, as the burning of fossil fuels is a primary driver of greenhouse gas emissions. However, integrating renewable energy sources such as solar, wind, and hydroelectric power into existing energy infrastructure poses significant challenges. Renewable energy is often intermittent, meaning that its generation fluctuates depending on weather conditions and time of day. AI can help manage this variability by predicting energy demand and supply patterns, optimizing the use of renewable resources, and ensuring grid stability.

AI-powered systems can forecast energy production from renewable sources, allowing utilities to better match supply with demand. For instance, machine learning models can predict the output of solar panels based on weather forecasts, ensuring that excess energy is stored or distributed during periods of high production. Similarly, AI can optimize the operation of wind turbines by adjusting their settings in response to changing wind conditions, maximizing energy production. In addition to renewable energy optimization, AI can contribute to energy efficiency by identifying areas of waste in energy consumption. Smart grids powered by AI can track energy usage in real time, automatically adjusting settings to reduce consumption during peak periods or when energy demand is low.

Furthermore, AI technologies are being employed in the design and operation of energy-efficient buildings. Smart building systems use AI to regulate heating, cooling, lighting, and ventilation based on occupancy patterns and external conditions. These systems learn from data over time, becoming more efficient in managing energy use while improving comfort for building occupants. This shift toward intelligent energy systems is essential for reducing carbon footprints, particularly in urban environments where energy consumption is highest. The convergence of AI and energy technologies creates a powerful tool for reducing emissions and improving the sustainability of energy infrastructure.

AI in Agriculture for Sustainable Food Production

Agriculture is another area where AI can make a substantial contribution to sustainability. Agriculture accounts for a significant portion of global greenhouse gas emissions, particularly through deforestation, methane emissions from livestock, and the use of synthetic fertilizers and pesticides. However, AI can help reduce the environmental impact of agriculture by promoting more efficient and sustainable farming practices. Precision agriculture, a field that relies heavily on AI, uses data-driven insights to optimize the use of resources such as water, fertilizers, and pesticides. AI systems can analyse data from soil sensors, satellite imagery, and drones to assess soil health, monitor crop growth, and predict the best times for planting and harvesting.

By leveraging AI, farmers can make more informed decisions about when and where to apply fertilizers or pesticides, reducing waste and minimizing the negative environmental effects of these chemicals. AI can also help optimize irrigation systems by predicting water needs based on weather forecasts, soil moisture levels, and crop requirements. This not only conserves water but also ensures that crops receive the optimal amount of moisture, leading to higher yields and better resource efficiency. In addition, AI can be used to monitor livestock health and well-being, predicting diseases or other health issues before they become major problems. This early detection allows for more efficient and humane management of animals, reducing the need for antibiotics and other harmful practices.

AI-driven innovations in agriculture are also addressing food security concerns by improving crop resilience to climate change. AI models can analyse genetic data to identify traits in crops that make them more resistant to extreme weather events such as droughts or floods. This information can guide the development of new crop varieties that are better suited to changing climatic conditions, ensuring a stable and sustainable food supply in the future. By optimizing the agricultural process and reducing its environmental impact, AI contributes to both climate change mitigation and the promotion of sustainable food systems.

Biodiversity Conservation and Ecosystem Management

Biodiversity loss is one of the most significant consequences of climate change, as rising temperatures, habitat destruction, and pollution threaten the survival of many species. AI plays a crucial role in biodiversity conservation by enabling the monitoring and protection of ecosystems and wildlife. Machine learning algorithms can analyse large datasets from environmental sensors, camera traps, and satellite imagery to track changes in biodiversity and identify areas that require conservation efforts. For example, AI-powered systems can detect and classify animal species in images, helping researchers monitor endangered species and track their movements without disturbing their natural habitats.

AI is also used in the study of ecosystems, where it can help model the impact of human activities and climate change on biodiversity. By analysing patterns in environmental data, AI can predict which species are most at risk of extinction due to changing climate conditions, deforestation, or habitat degradation. This enables targeted conservation efforts and the allocation of resources to areas where they can have the greatest impact. Furthermore, AI can assist in reforestation projects by identifying the best areas to plant trees and predicting the long-term success of these initiatives based on factors such as soil quality, climate conditions, and biodiversity.

In addition to its role in monitoring and protecting biodiversity, AI is being used to develop solutions for ecosystem restoration. For example, AI systems can analyse satellite images to assess the health of coral reefs, identifying areas that are suffering from bleaching or other stressors. This data can inform restoration strategies and help track the progress of efforts to revive damaged ecosystems. By integrating AI into biodiversity conservation, we can make more informed decisions that protect and restore the natural systems on which life depends.

Waste Management and Circular Economy

AI is also contributing to sustainability through innovations in waste management and the promotion of a circular economy. The global waste crisis, driven by excessive consumption and inefficient disposal methods, is a significant environmental challenge. AI technologies can enhance recycling processes, making them more efficient and reducing the amount of waste sent to landfills. AI-powered robots and sorting systems are already being used in recycling plants to automate the separation of different types of materials, improving the accuracy and speed of sorting and reducing human error. These systems can identify and sort materials such as plastics, metals, and paper based on their unique properties, leading to higher-quality recycled materials and reducing the need for virgin resources.

Additionally, AI is enabling the development of waste reduction strategies by identifying patterns in consumption and waste production. Machine learning algorithms can analyse data on consumer behaviour, helping businesses optimize product design and packaging to reduce waste. AI is also being used to improve waste-to-energy technologies, where waste materials are converted into energy through processes like anaerobic digestion or incineration. By optimizing these processes, AI can help reduce emissions from landfills and decrease the environmental impact of waste disposal.

The transition to a circular economy, where resources are reused, refurbished, and recycled, is a key component of sustainability. AI plays a crucial role in this transition by improving resource management, streamlining supply chains, and enabling more efficient product design. AI-powered platforms can track the lifecycle of products, from production to disposal, allowing businesses to make more sustainable decisions and reduce waste generation. By enhancing waste management systems and supporting the circular economy, AI contributes to the goal of reducing humanity's ecological footprint and promoting more sustainable consumption patterns.

Conclusion

Artificial intelligence is playing an increasingly important role in addressing the challenges posed by climate change and advancing sustainability efforts. Through its applications in climate modelling, energy efficiency, agriculture, biodiversity conservation, and waste management, AI has the potential to drive significant improvements in how we understand and interact with the environment. By leveraging data, machine learning algorithms, and automation, AI helps optimize resource use, reduce emissions, and create more resilient systems that can adapt to the changing climate. While AI is not a panacea for all environmental issues, it is a powerful tool that, when combined with other technological and policy solutions, can play a pivotal role in creating a more sustainable and climate-resilient future. As AI continues to evolve, its potential to address the urgent environmental challenges facing our planet will only increase, offering new opportunities for innovation and progress in the fight against climate change.

AI solutions for environmental monitoring

Artificial Intelligence (AI) is rapidly becoming a critical tool in addressing environmental challenges, offering a wide range of solutions for environmental monitoring. With the growing concerns over climate change, deforestation, pollution, and loss of biodiversity, the ability to track, predict, and mitigate these issues through AI is more important than ever. AI can process vast amounts of data quickly and accurately, which is especially important when it comes to monitoring and analysing complex environmental systems that involve numerous variables. From air and water quality to wildlife conservation, AI applications are revolutionizing the way we understand and manage our planet's resources.

One of the most impactful ways AI is contributing to environmental monitoring is through the analysis of sensor data for air and water quality. With the proliferation of IoT (Internet of Things) devices, real-time data from air quality sensors, weather stations, and water quality monitoring systems are being collected at an unprecedented scale. AI algorithms are capable of analysing this data to detect patterns, identify potential risks, and even predict future trends, such as air pollution spikes or water contamination events. Machine learning models can process this data in real-time, providing valuable insights to policymakers, environmental agencies, and communities, enabling them to take preventive actions. For instance, AI can detect the early signs of hazardous pollutants, like particulate matter or harmful chemicals in water sources, allowing authorities to respond swiftly and mitigate health risks.

AI is also being applied in satellite remote sensing for environmental monitoring. Satellites equipped with advanced sensors can capture vast amounts of data about land use, forest cover, ocean temperatures, and atmospheric conditions. AI models can be used to analyse satellite imagery, enabling the detection of environmental changes over time. For example, AI can track deforestation rates in real time, monitor crop health for agricultural planning, and assess the impact of climate change on polar ice caps or coastal areas. AI can even assist in identifying illegal activities such as illegal logging or poaching by analysing patterns in satellite imagery that may not be visible to the human eye. This ability to automate the analysis of large-scale satellite data allows for more frequent monitoring of environmental conditions, making it possible to respond faster to environmental crises.

Another significant application of AI in environmental monitoring is in biodiversity and wildlife conservation. AI-powered technologies are being used to monitor ecosystems and track the movement of endangered species. Using camera traps, drones, and acoustic sensors, AI can process images and sounds from the environment to detect and identify species, count populations, and assess habitat health. AI algorithms can differentiate between species with remarkable accuracy, even in challenging environments like dense forests or remote areas. These systems can automatically alert conservationists to any anomalies, such as the sudden disappearance of a species from a particular region or the presence of invasive species that threaten local biodiversity. In addition to direct monitoring, AI is also being used to model species migration patterns, predict future habitat changes, and assess the impact of human activity on ecosystems. This data-driven approach enhances conservation efforts by enabling more targeted and efficient interventions.

AI is also a powerful tool for predicting the impact of climate change and natural disasters. Climate models that simulate long-term environmental changes can be enhanced with machine learning algorithms, which can process large datasets and offer more accurate predictions. These predictions are essential for disaster preparedness, as they can provide insights into the likelihood and timing of events such as hurricanes, wildfires, or floods. In the case of wildfires, for example, AI can process data from weather conditions, vegetation types, and historical fire patterns to predict where and when a fire is most likely to occur. This information can be used by emergency services to pre-emptively allocate resources and issue evacuation warnings. Similarly, AI can predict areas at high risk for flooding, allowing cities to strengthen infrastructure and improve resilience to natural disasters. The ability to forecast environmental risks with greater precision can help mitigate the effects of climate change and protect vulnerable populations.

In addition to predictive modelling, AI is also being applied to optimize resource management in sectors like agriculture and water usage. Precision agriculture, which uses AI to optimize crop yields while minimizing the environmental impact, is one of the most promising applications of AI in environmental sustainability. By analysing data from drones, sensors, and satellite imagery, AI can help farmers monitor soil moisture, track pest populations, and predict the best times to plant or harvest crops. AI algorithms can also identify areas where water is being used inefficiently and recommend adjustments to irrigation schedules. This helps conserve water resources while maximizing agricultural output. Furthermore, AI can assist in reducing the environmental impact of farming by identifying methods for reducing pesticide use and improving crop rotation strategies, thus promoting soil health and biodiversity.

Water management is another area where AI is making a significant impact. With the increasing demand for water and the challenges posed by climate change, it is essential to manage water resources efficiently. AI is being used to monitor and optimize water distribution networks, detect leaks in pipes, and predict periods of water scarcity. Through the integration of sensor networks and machine learning, AI can provide real-time analysis of water quality and availability, helping municipalities and water utilities make informed decisions. Additionally, AI can assist in the design and implementation of sustainable irrigation systems, which are crucial for agriculture in regions prone to droughts. By improving the efficiency of water use, AI can help ensure that this vital resource is conserved and distributed equitably.

AI is also transforming waste management systems. Using machine learning algorithms, AI can optimize waste collection routes, identify recycling patterns, and improve the sorting of recyclable materials. Smart waste bins equipped with sensors can alert waste management companies when they are full, enabling more efficient collection schedules. Additionally, AI is being used to improve the recycling process itself by developing automated sorting systems that can identify and separate distinct types of materials more accurately than humans. This is crucial for increasing recycling rates and reducing the amount of waste that ends up in landfills. AI can also help identify trends in waste generation, enabling municipalities to implement waste reduction strategies and promote more sustainable consumption patterns among citizens.

Despite the tremendous potential of AI for environmental monitoring, there are challenges and limitations to consider. One of the key concerns is the availability and quality of data. While AI can process vast amounts of data, it requires high-quality, reliable information to generate accurate insights. In many regions, particularly in developing countries, access to environmental data is limited, and the infrastructure to collect and process this data may not be in place. Additionally, AI models are only as good as the data they are trained on, and biased or incomplete datasets can lead to inaccurate predictions or decisions. Ensuring that AI systems are trained on diverse, representative datasets and that data privacy concerns are addressed is essential for the responsible use of AI in environmental monitoring.

Another challenge is the need for collaboration between different stakeholders, including governments, businesses, scientists, and communities. Effective environmental monitoring requires the integration of data from various sources, such as satellite imagery, sensor networks, and field observations. Collaboration across sectors is necessary to ensure that AI systems are developed and deployed in ways that benefit society as a whole. Additionally, there is a need for regulatory frameworks and policies that promote the responsible use of AI while addressing ethical concerns, such as transparency, accountability, and the potential displacement of jobs in traditional industries.

Despite these challenges, AI has the potential to transform environmental monitoring and contribute to the sustainable management of our planet's resources. By harnessing the power of AI, we can gain a deeper understanding of environmental changes, predict future risks, and take initiative-taking measures to protect our ecosystems and communities. As AI technology continues to evolve, it is likely that its applications in environmental monitoring will expand, offering even more innovative solutions to the pressing environmental challenges we face today.

Smart grids and energy efficiency

Smart grids and energy efficiency are key components of the modern electrical infrastructure and have become central to efforts aimed at addressing the world's growing energy demands, improving energy sustainability, and reducing environmental impact. As the global population increases and energy consumption continues to rise, the transition from traditional electrical grids to smart grids has become a necessary step to meet these challenges. Smart grids utilize digital technology to monitor and manage the flow of electricity across a wide area, offering a dynamic and flexible approach to energy distribution and consumption. This advanced technology enables two-way communication between utilities and consumers, which is a significant departure from the one-way flow of electricity characteristic of traditional grids.

A major goal of smart grids is to enhance the efficiency and reliability of energy systems. Through the use of sensors, advanced metering, and automated systems, smart grids can detect and respond to changes in electricity demand in real time. This ability to dynamically adjust power flow is essential for optimizing energy efficiency, reducing waste, and lowering operational costs. By integrating renewable energy sources, such as solar, wind, and hydroelectric power, smart grids can also contribute to a cleaner energy mix. Since renewable energy sources are often intermittent, meaning they do not produce a constant flow of power, smart grids help balance supply and demand by storing energy during times of low demand and releasing it when needed, a process known as demand response.

The integration of smart grid technology also offers significant benefits to consumers. With smart meters and real-time monitoring, consumers gain more control over their energy usage. They can track energy consumption patterns, receive immediate feedback on their usage, and adjust their habits accordingly to save energy and reduce costs. This level of transparency and control encourages more energy-efficient behaviour, which can result in lower utility bills and a reduction in the overall environmental footprint of households and businesses. Additionally, by encouraging the use of energy-efficient appliances, lighting, and heating/cooling systems, smart grids help further optimize energy consumption.

Another key feature of smart grids is their ability to improve grid reliability and resilience. Traditional electrical grids are often vulnerable to disruptions caused by weather events, equipment failures, and other unforeseen circumstances. In contrast, smart grids can self-heal by automatically detecting faults and rerouting power to minimize outages. This initiative-taking approach to grid management ensures that electricity delivery is more consistent, reduces downtime, and enhances the overall security of the energy system. By using predictive analytics, smart grids can also forecast energy demand and supply imbalances, allowing utilities to take preventative measures before problems occur. This predictive capability further improves energy efficiency by preventing the waste of resources and ensuring that the right amount of energy is generated and distributed.

As we transition to cleaner and more sustainable energy sources, energy efficiency is not just about saving money, but also about reducing the environmental impact of energy production. The traditional approach to energy generation relies heavily on fossil fuels, which are responsible for significant greenhouse gas emissions and pollution. Smart grids facilitate the integration of renewable energy into the grid, which helps reduce dependence on fossil fuels and decrease overall carbon emissions. For instance, during periods of low energy demand, excess renewable energy can be stored or redirected, ensuring that it is used effectively rather than wasted. This is especially important as the world works toward achieving international climate goals, such as those outlined in the Paris Agreement, which calls for a substantial reduction in global carbon emissions.

Energy efficiency and sustainability are not only about large-scale infrastructure changes but also involve encouraging individual actions that contribute to the overall goal of reducing energy consumption. Smart grids support this by enabling the development of energy-efficient homes and businesses. Through the use of smart appliances, intelligent lighting systems, and home energy management systems, individuals can reduce their energy usage without sacrificing comfort or convenience. For example, smart thermostats can learn a household's heating and cooling preferences and adjust temperature settings automatically to minimize energy use. Similarly, smart lighting systems can be programmed to adjust brightness levels based on ambient light conditions or occupancy, further reducing unnecessary energy consumption.

One of the challenges in implementing smart grid technology, however, is the need for significant investment in infrastructure. The installation of smart meters, sensors, and other advanced technologies can be costly, particularly in regions where the electrical grid is outdated or in developing countries with limited resources. Additionally, the integration of renewable energy sources and energy storage systems requires substantial upfront investment. Despite these challenges, the long-term benefits of smart grids—such as improved energy efficiency, reduced operational costs, and lower environmental impact—make the investment worthwhile. Governments and utilities are increasingly recognizing the value of smart grids, and many have already begun to roll out pilot projects and large-scale deployments.

Another consideration is data security and privacy. As smart grids rely on real-time data transmission and analysis, there is a need to ensure that this data is protected from cyberattacks and unauthorized access. Personal consumption data, which can provide insights into a household's energy habits, must be safeguarded to protect consumer privacy. To address these concerns, utilities and governments must invest in robust cybersecurity measures and ensure that smart grid systems comply with data protection regulations.

In conclusion, smart grids represent a significant advancement in the way electricity is generated, distributed, and consumed. They offer a more efficient, reliable, and sustainable energy system that can meet the demands of a growing global population while also addressing environmental concerns. Through the integration of renewable energy sources, real-time monitoring, and demand response, smart grids help optimize energy efficiency, reduce waste, and lower operational costs. They also provide consumers with greater control over their energy usage, encouraging energy-efficient behaviour and reducing overall energy consumption. While there are challenges in terms of cost and data security, the long-term benefits of smart grids make them a critical component of a sustainable energy future. As technology continues to evolve, smart grids will play an increasingly important role in helping to create a more sustainable and energy-efficient world.

Risks and challenges of AI's environmental impact

The environmental impact of Artificial Intelligence (AI) is an increasingly important topic in the discourse around technology and sustainability. As AI technologies continue to evolve and expand across various sectors, the environmental risks and challenges associated with their use are becoming more pronounced. These risks are primarily tied to the energy consumption required for the development, deployment, and operation of AI systems, as well as the potential for electronic waste (e-waste) generated by AI hardware. AI models, particularly deep learning algorithms, require significant computational power, which in turn leads to high energy demands. Data centres, which house the computational infrastructure for AI, consume vast amounts of electricity, much of which is still sourced from fossil fuels in many parts of the world. This energy consumption contributes to carbon emissions, further exacerbating global climate change. Furthermore, the development of AI models often requires massive datasets, which necessitate substantial energy for data storage and processing. These processes, although invisible to the end user, have a considerable carbon footprint that is frequently overlooked in the conversations about AI's benefits.

The computational demands of AI are not limited to the research and development phase; they extend to the operational phase as well. Many AI applications, such as natural language processing models or computer vision systems, rely on continuous, real-time data processing, further intensifying their energy needs. For example, large language models like GPT-4 require enormous computational power for training and inference, with each iteration consuming vast amounts of energy. In addition, the expansion of AI technologies in consumer devices, such as smart speakers, autonomous vehicles, and Internet of Things (IoT) devices, requires ongoing power consumption. The cumulative effect of these energy demands can be significant, especially as the deployment of AI technologies continues to grow across various industries. In some cases, AI may exacerbate environmental challenges, such as the increased use of AI in the production and operation of autonomous vehicles, which, while offering benefits like improved traffic flow and safety, also increase the demand for energy-intensive infrastructure and create additional waste through the production of specialized hardware.

Another environmental challenge posed by AI is the lifecycle of the hardware that supports these technologies. AI systems rely on high-performance computing hardware, including processors, GPUs (Graphics Processing Units), and specialized chips designed for AI workloads. The manufacturing of these devices requires the extraction of rare earth metals and other raw materials, which can have significant environmental consequences. The mining of these materials can result in habitat destruction, pollution, and the depletion of non-renewable resources. In addition, the energy-intensive process of manufacturing and transporting these devices further compounds their environmental impact. Once the hardware reaches the end of its useful life, it contributes to the growing global problem of e-waste. E-waste, which consists of discarded electronic devices, is one of the fastest-growing waste streams worldwide. Much of this waste is not properly recycled or disposed of, leading to soil and water contamination from hazardous substances such as lead, mercury, and cadmium. The short lifespan of many AI devices, coupled with the rapid pace of technological obsolescence, results in a constant cycle of production and disposal that exacerbates the strain on the environment.

In addition to the direct environmental impacts of AI, there are also indirect consequences associated with the broader adoption of AI-driven systems. For instance, AI has the potential to drive increased demand for automation in industries like manufacturing, agriculture, and logistics. While automation may lead to improved efficiency and reduced waste in some cases, it could also lead to the overproduction of goods and increased resource consumption. AI-driven optimization in supply chains, for example, might reduce transportation emissions by streamlining routes and improving inventory management, but it could also result in higher levels of production, creating a rebound effect that ultimately increases the environmental footprint of these industries. Moreover, AI technologies have the potential to amplify unsustainable practices in industries that already have a high environmental impact. For instance, AI could be used to optimize processes in fossil fuel extraction, increasing production and prolonging the lifespan of non-renewable energy sources, thereby hindering efforts to transition to cleaner energy alternatives.

One of the most significant challenges in addressing the environmental impact of AI is the lack of standardized metrics and transparency around energy consumption and emissions. Unlike industries such as transportation or manufacturing, where carbon footprints are more easily quantifiable, AI's environmental impact is often opaque and difficult to measure. AI research papers and industry reports typically focus on the accuracy or efficiency of AI models, with little attention paid to the environmental costs associated with training and deploying these models. The energy consumption of data centres, for example, is often not disclosed, and there are few industry-wide standards for reporting AI's carbon footprint. This lack of transparency makes it difficult for policymakers, researchers, and consumers to make informed decisions about the sustainability of AI technologies. As AI continues to evolve, there is an urgent need for standardized metrics and reporting frameworks that can help track and reduce the environmental impact of these systems. Additionally, AI developers and organizations must prioritize sustainability by adopting energy-efficient practices and leveraging renewable energy sources to power their operations.

Despite these challenges, there are several potential solutions and strategies that can mitigate the environmental impact of AI. One of the most promising approaches is the development of more energy-efficient AI algorithms and hardware. Researchers are exploring ways to design AI models that require less computational power to achieve similar or even better results. For example, techniques like pruning, quantization, and knowledge distillation can be used to reduce the size of AI models without compromising their performance. Advances in hardware design, such as the development of specialized AI chips that consume less power, also hold promise for reducing the environmental footprint of AI systems. Additionally, the use of renewable energy sources to power data centres and AI infrastructure can significantly reduce the carbon footprint of these technologies. Some leading tech companies have already made commitments to achieve carbon neutrality by transitioning to renewable energy and offsetting their emissions, and these efforts could serve as a model for others in the industry.

Moreover, AI itself has the potential to contribute to environmental sustainability by enabling more efficient use of resources in various sectors. For example, AI can be used to optimize energy consumption in buildings, improve agricultural practices, and reduce waste in manufacturing processes. By leveraging AI to enhance sustainability efforts, industries can reduce their environmental impact and make strides toward achieving a more sustainable future. AI-driven solutions, such as predictive maintenance in manufacturing, smart grids for energy distribution, and AI-powered climate modelling, could help mitigate some of the environmental challenges posed by human activity. However, these solutions must be developed and implemented in a way that prioritizes long-term sustainability and minimizes unintended negative consequences.

In conclusion, while AI has the potential to drive significant positive changes in society, its environmental impact must be carefully managed to avoid exacerbating existing environmental challenges. The risks and challenges associated with AI's environmental footprint are tied to its energy consumption, hardware lifecycle, and potential to drive increased resource demand. Addressing these challenges requires a multifaceted approach that includes the development of energy-efficient AI algorithms, the adoption of renewable energy sources, and greater transparency around the environmental impact of AI systems. By prioritizing sustainability in the development and deployment of AI technologies, we can ensure that AI contributes to a more sustainable future rather than becoming a driver of environmental degradation.